THE SPIRIT OF MY HAIR

THE SPIRIT OF MY HAIR

Reclaiming Identity, Heritage, and Pride
through the Story of Black Hair

GUYLAINE CONQUET

 Just Afro Publishing

The Spirit of My Hair
Reclaiming Identity, Heritage, and Pride through the Story of Black Hair
©2025 Guylaine Conquet. All Rights Reserved.
Published by Just Afro Publishing

Printed in the United States of America

Dedication

To my children,
Alicia, Gregory, and Jordan—
my three North Stars.
Every page is a love letter
to your courage, your laughter, and your light.

To my buddies,
Céline and Sonia—
thank you for cheering me on
even when I searched for excuses not to write.

To my family, my roots,
and my steadfast supporters in Guadeloupe.

To the one who believed in me,
and to the schools, colleges, universities,
art galleries, and museums
that gave me a voice and welcomed my story
I am forever grateful.

To those who love my art
and carry a piece of my journey on their walls
you inspire me to keep creating.

To everyone who has walked with me
on this hair journey,
and helped me understand my purpose
your faith made this book possible.

Team France, Team USA, Team UK,
and soon Team Africa and Team Asia
thank you for opening doors, hearts, and homes
across oceans.

I LOVE YOU, MY PEOPLE.

Message from ABOUBACAR TRAORÉ, former Air France flight attendant whose story sparked the French Hair Discrimination Bill

Hair, a mirror of our identities, is also the scene of insidious discrimination.

Beyond the right to be different, I defend the right to indifference: the right not to be judged, classified, or rejected for what grows naturally on our heads.

Our hair should never be a reason for exclusion or hierarchy.

This book is a further step towards this collective awareness.

It's not just about tolerance, it's about respect.

And respect begins with indifference to differences.

Preface

As an African Diaspora Studies scholar whose research focuses on ways Afro descendants express their identities through the arts, I find Guylaine Conquet's book a welcome addition to the literary landscape. *The Spirit of My Hair* is not just an autobiography, but a resourceful volume for North Americans and United States residents interested in the Black experience outside US borders. Conquet was born in the French-speaking Caribbean island of Guadeloupe. She grew up in Lyon, France and moved to the US in 2017. She now calls Atlanta home. The author brings to the North American context a very important component of the Black experience that is lost sight of in this country. There is no monopoly on Blackness. It is as multiple as the slave routes which uprooted Africans from their homelands and transplanted them everywhere across the globe. There are varied strands of Blackness. Conquet's is Francophone. When I read her manuscript, I couldn't help but think of Guadeloupean writer Maryse Condé's novel *The Last of the African Kings*. Precisely, the encounter between Guadeloupeans/Antilleans and African Americans is at the center of Condé's chronicle.

Two years ago, based on her artwork and advocacy against hair discrimination, I invited Conquet to be in conversation with Spelman College students. After her talk on campus, many of my students established a correlation between her work and the concepts of racial identity formation, unfinished migration, framing and defining diaspora, and knowledge construction, pedagogy of the oppressed and critical consciousness in the short reflective essay they wrote.

Later that same year, the author and I attended a symposium on new Francophone Caribbean perspectives at the University of

Pittsburgh where I read a paper and she exhibited her art. Since then, her art practice has matured exponentially, and she has done extensive research on discrimination based on hair texture, which constitutes the basis of her painting. Her activism was critical in introducing legislation against hair harassment in France for the first time. She has expanded her interest in natural hair to include the damages of pressed hair at the intersection of economic disenfranchisement and medical impoverishment.

Conquet's biography is a story of transformation, a journey as she puts it "that began with a paintbrush, a decision to tell my story and a refusal to let fear win." More than just hair, the book is about transformation, the reclaiming of her identity. Find out how "(my) painting gave me a platform to talk about hair discrimination. My research gave me credibility to speak to lawmakers. My lived experience gave me authenticity that couldn't be questioned. But most importantly, my willingness to be vulnerable, to share my pain and my healing publicly, created connections with other people who had lived similar experiences."

Alix Pierre, Ph.D., African Diaspora and the World, Spelman College and Resident Scholar, Diaspora Vibe Cultural Arts Incubator

Table of Contents

Chapter 1: The Seeds of Rejection

My earliest memories are painted in the warm colors of the Island of Guadeloupe in the French West Indies—the smells, children playing marbles, the sound of water carriers balancing their loads on their heads, and the daily rhythm of life in our close-knit neighborhood. It wasn't a wealthy area, but it was rich with love and community. Every day at sunset, the entire neighborhood would quiet down. People would clean themselves, then gather on their porches and balconies to share stories and chat as the day drew to a close.

On one particular day, it was stiflingly hot, almost unreal, as if the air itself were reluctant to move. I was lying on the hot cement of the patio in our Nérée neighborhood in Les Abymes, watching the corrugated sheet metal ceiling and lost in thought, when a raucous honk broke the silence. Not a car horn—a fishmonger's horn. Every vendor on our street had their own distinctive sound, but this one was long, dragging, a little tired, announcing fresh fish.

Five years old, I looked up curiously. My grandmother had crossed the street, and I already knew from the way voices were being raised that a verbal joust was in progress. I didn't need to see to know who was commanding the scene.

"Tousa lajan pou dé twa ti pwason!"* she shouted, hands firmly planted on her hips. She gestured with natural authority, speaking in a mixture of Creole and indignant sighs, glaring at the poor merchant. He wanted to sell his fish at the daily price; she wanted catfish, and certainly not at that price.

Everyone called her Man Marcel, though her real name was Mercedes. She was known as the wife of Marcel Conquet, following the old custom where women took on their husband's first name with "Man" in front. I never understood this tradition. Perhaps it was a form of respect, or perhaps it was simply the way of saying that in each family, the husband was considered the head. But watching her negotiate, there was no question who truly held the power in those moments.

The merchant sighed and gave in, as they all did eventually. I didn't yet know what diplomacy was, but I was silently learning the Guadeloupean art of negotiation. That fish, once conquered through her fierce bargaining, would end up a few hours later in a large stew pot, transformed into a thick, rich court bouillon seasoned with spices and hot peppers, served alongside slices of breadfruit that melted like butter on the tongue.

My grandmother was an extraordinary woman who took care of us while my mother was away in France. She was dark-skinned, with a strong character that commanded respect or dislike throughout our neighborhood. Some people were even afraid of her, but to me, she was everything. I can still see her silhouette in the sweltering midday light.

Her face, soft and sculptural, bore the beauty of our Caribbean women. Her body, firm and solid, bore witness to a life of toil. Thirteen children, days spent walking, washing, feeding, consoling... and yet she was upright and dignified.

She always wore that flowery, light cotton apron dress, the colors of which had faded with age. The fullness of the fabric hinted at a petticoat carefully tucked underneath, a discreet but essential detail for her, handed down by her elders. She dressed as if perpetuating a ritual.

Her hands, gnarled and powerful, rested on her hips, her straw hat braided, wide and worn, a faithful companion against sunburn. I remember the way she would always replace it with a precise gesture, frowning in annoyance.

She was supportive, loving, kind, and an incredible cook whose food seemed almost religious in its perfection. She used colorful Creole sayings to illustrate her points, and in my childhood head, I imagined what they meant in real life. "Lé chyen ka japé pa ké" (when the dog barks by the tail), she would say, and I smiled as I imagined a dog barking by the tail, which meant that the place was so far away, it was almost inaccessible. She was a woman who stood her ground. I gained my fortitude from my grandmother. This woman, without a doubt, influenced me.

I was a bright child, advanced for my age. By preschool, I could already read, my letters came easily to me, and the teachers, whom we called aunties, were impressed by this little girl who seemed to absorb knowledge so quickly. I was vibrant and happy, though quiet by nature, living with my grandmother. My mother was a part of the BUMIDOM program in France. It was a government project established in 1963 to facilitate the mass migration of young Caribbean people from France's overseas territories to work in French hospitals, post offices, and administrative roles where labor was needed. They said it addressed the unemployment problem in Guadeloupe, Martinique, Réunion, and French Guiana. Although the intent of the program was good, often the Black French Caribbeans would be treated as second-class citizens in France.

The sounds of our neighborhood were the soundtrack of my childhood. In this neighborhood, where each family carried its own history, some places were very special, almost sacred to us: the Trois Chemins de Nérée Abymes and the Romage family's house, which was our neighbor's. This was where the heart of the neighborhood beat—literally and figuratively. As soon as the drums of Gwoka, the traditional music inherited from our African ancestors, resonated, everything changed.

The drum wasn't just an instrument: it was a language, a weapon, a breath. And among the Romage family, this memory had never been silenced.

From the first sounds, a shiver ran through me. Although I was a child, my body vibrated to the music, and an irresistible urge to dance gripped me. My heart instinctively tuned to this rhythm. I was captivated. It was as if the ancestors were watching over this place, as if their voices, their pain, their songs still floated in the air.

I would slip discreetly onto the veranda, a fascinated little intruder, to listen to these powerful, soulful songs and spy on the crowd that came for this event. They spoke of courage, love, freedom, broken chains, and hopes still alive.

I didn't always understand all the words, but I felt everything. Some of the women would perform the Gwoka dance, a rhythmic African-inspired dance that expresses joy, gratitude, and pride. They would move their legs and hips to the beat of the drums and percussion. In some of the moves, it would appear that they would tip over, but they'd bounce back up quickly, still in sync with the music. It's called the Bigidi. It was a reminder that no matter what Black people face, they'd always bounce back and persevere. There was magic in those moments. A silent communion. A memory transmitted, from the singing to the drum beat to my heart. The Gwoka wasn't a performance: it was a collective breath.

Each beat murmured: "Nou la," which means "we are here." And I, a little child, was there too.

My grandmother didn't approve of this music, calling it "old kind of negro music," but I was drawn to it. My grandmother's household included my younger sister, aged three, and several cousins whose mothers had also gone to France for work. The older cousins looked after us, the younger ones, creating a web of family care that felt secure and loving. I lived with my grandmother and grandfather for a few years. My grandfather spent his days in the fields growing sugar cane and yams and raising oxen. I especially remember my cousins and I waiting for his return, like the Messiah, to enjoy juicy mangoes and genips.

My father was largely absent from my life—he had married another woman after I was born. My stepmother was a light-skinned woman with long hair, and during my rare visits, she would make comments about my hair, comparing it to "koko sek" (dry coconut). Her words made me feel like a rejected outcast. On a few occasions, I stayed with dad's mother instead to avoid the ridicule.

My hair during those early years was nothing spectacular—thin and fine, styled in small braids with little barrettes that I loved to wear to school. At school, the rules were strict: only braids were allowed. Loose hair? Not allowed. Cornrows? Not yet known. You had to be "well coiffed," in other words, compliant and disciplined. On the playground, hierarchy was based on the length of your braids. The longer they were, the more popular you were. My braids weren't very big, but they were my pride and joy, decorated with satin bows that were often colorful and sometimes matched my dress.

At home, having my hair done was part of everyday life. It was an ordinary moment, full of complicity, yet dreaded. Those who did it were often moms, big sisters, or neighbors. For me, it was mostly my cousins and our close neighbor, Ginette. She enjoyed combing my hair as if I were her doll. For me, it was a torture session. Sitting on the floor or on a bench wedged between the firm thighs of my hairdresser, I would look up at the ceiling, teeth clenched. Before braiding, there was the famous greasing stage: Vaseline or black castor oil to try to soften my bush.

Then came the comb—too fine for our hair texture, but we used it anyway, determined to make our parts straight and our hair combed out. It hooked, it pulled, it stuck. And if I moved or moaned, a pat on the head would call me to order: "Hold still!" I was simply told that I wasn't lucky enough to have "good" hair. I wanted to look pretty like the other girls, adorned with the small ornaments that Caribbean girls traditionally wore to school.

In my childhood memories, my grandmother often wore her hair in a style we called "choux" (flats, Bantu knots). On Sundays at church, the women competed in elegance with their hats. For everyday errands, she, like many adults, wrapped her head with a square of madras, the bright plaid cloth that came from the city of Madras (now Chennai) in India. After slavery in the French Caribbean Islands ended in 1848, they brought in East Indians for labor to replace the slaves. Traders carried the madras to the Caribbean earlier, in the seventeenth century. Light and sturdy, it suited the tropical heat.

Over time, madras was embraced by local people, including the enslaved and their descendants, who folded it into their culture. It became a symbol of identity and quiet resistance, a meeting point of African and Indian influences.

From that cloth, women shaped headwraps of knots, pleats, and careful drapes. They were artwork, proof of Black women's eye for beauty and invention. Much later, when I began studying hairstyles, I discovered that these wraps also had a voice. They held social meaning. They could hint at a woman's mood or marital status.

Common styles and what people read in them:

- One point showing: heart free.
- Two points: interested, but you may try your luck.
- Three points: taken, married.

- Four points: room for the bold.
- The "chaudière": a ceremonial wrap with diagonal pleats.

Sometimes I watched Man Marcel do her hair. She kept a wide-tooth comb, a bottle of black castor oil, and a simple hairpin. With those, she formed her tight little choux. I wanted choux too, or caca cabrit, small coiled buns we loved. I was too young. At school, they were not allowed. Only braids were permitted.

I didn't know it yet, but my hair adventures were far from over. What I was experiencing was only a prelude. Soon, my mother, who lived in France, would return to Guadeloupe to take my sister and me back with her. Like so many other Guadeloupeans who had left under the BUMIDOM program, their children would soon join them. And now it was our turn to change our lives, our climate, our culture... and the way we saw ourselves.

I was thrilled! France represented paradise to us, a world entirely different from our own. We would have cars, public transportation, an apartment, and all the wonders of modern life. It was January when we left, the middle of winter, and my mother brought us big warm clothes to wear. I remember trying on a pleated mini skirt and a fur-lined jacket in tartan fabric. It was my first time in heavy winter clothing. My sister and I were beside ourselves with excitement.

But before we even left Guadeloupe, my mother made a decision that would mark the beginning of my complicated relationship with my appearance. She took us to have our hair cut short—very short. Her reasoning was practical: she worked long hours at the hospital on staggered shifts, from seven in the morning sometimes until her night shift ended at nine in the evening, and she wouldn't have time to comb our hair. She didn't know how to care for it properly anyway, she said.

I remember sitting in that chair, watching my hair fall to the floor in dark clumps. The feeling was terrible—a deep sadness that seemed to settle in my chest. When I touched my head afterward, I felt almost nothing. My hair had been thin to begin with, and now, cut so short, I looked practically bald. The mirror reflected someone I didn't recognize.

The reaction when I returned to my grandmother's house was devastating. My cousins, my uncles, the whole extended family gathered around, and their words cut deep: "Oh, look at her. She looks like a boy." At that time, people didn't hesitate to speak their minds, regardless of how their words might impact a child. The shame I felt in that moment was profound—a six-year-old girl being told she looked like a boy, standing there with my shorn head, feeling exposed and different in the worst possible way.

In my young mind, I had now entered the category of "untouchables." I was cruelly mocked for my hair, and it was all rooted in ignorance. So many hurtful expressions, often borrowed from the animal or plant world, that reduced frizzy hair to something wild, shapeless, undesirable.

These words, which were used casually, nonetheless carried a muted violence. Like many other attributes inherited from our African origins, our hair was perceived as a burden, a shame to be hidden and corrected.

This was my introduction to the concept that there was something wrong with my natural appearance, something that needed to be managed, controlled, or changed. I didn't understand it then, but those seeds of self-doubt and rejection were being planted, ready to grow in the foreign soil of France, where I would soon discover what it truly meant to be different.

As we prepared to leave for our new life, I carried with me the warmth of my grandmother's love, the rhythms of Gwoka music, and the memory of the community that had shaped my earliest years. But I also carried something else, a new awareness of my hair, my appearance, and the way others perceived me. The little girl who had been confident and bright in Guadeloupe was about to encounter a world where being different wasn't just noticed, it was questioned, examined, and often rejected.

The plane to France would take us far from Guadeloupe. I was excited for the adventure ahead, but I was also unknowingly carrying the first wounds that would shape how I saw myself for years to come. Here I was, at six years old, diving into the unknown—fear and excitement intermingled, feeling privileged while my cousins who came after looked at me with envy, a small victory in my young mind.

When we arrived in Lyon, the reality of our new life began to unfold in ways I hadn't anticipated. We arrived in the middle of the school year with no time to recover from jet lag or acclimate. The next day, we headed to the small school of Guilloux in Saint-Genis-Laval. My sister was placed in kindergarten, and I was in primary school. My mother enrolled us, and I remember that first walk through the school gates. I entered a world that was completely foreign to me. Not just because I was in a new country, but also because, as I looked around the playground, the hallways, and the classrooms, I realized I was the only Black child in the entire school.

The stares began immediately. Children would stop their conversations mid-sentence to watch us pass. Some would point, others would whisper behind cupped hands. But it was when they began to speak directly to us that the real education in otherness began.

"Are you African?" they would ask, as if the word itself carried some mysterious weight. When I tried to explain that we were from Guadeloupe, a French territory, their faces would scrunch in confusion. The geography lesson was lost on them—in their minds, Black skin meant Africa, and Africa meant something savage and foreign that they had only seen in books or on television. In their eyes, I should almost have appeared in a jute loincloth.

The questions about my hair were relentless. Even though it was cut short, they were fascinated by its texture. "Why is your hair so woolly?" they would ask, reaching out to touch it without permission, as if I were some kind of exhibit in a museum or zoo. These weren't necessarily malicious children, but their innocent curiosity felt like tiny daggers, each question reinforcing that I was different, that I was other, that I didn't belong.

The teasing escalated as days turned into weeks. Comments about my "Black skin" were delivered with a mixture of fascination and mockery. Some children would make jokes, others would simply stare as if they couldn't quite figure out what I was. The combination of my shorn hair and my skin color seemed to make me an object of endless curiosity and, increasingly, ridicule.

What frustrated me most was their attitude and the sheer ignorance in their assumptions and questions. I was six years old, but even at that age, I could sense the absurdity of their beliefs about Africa, about Black people, about me. I wanted to shake them, to explain that I was just like them—a child who played, who learned, who had feelings. I wished desperately that they could see me as a human being, not as some exotic specimen to be examined and questioned.

I used to stare blankly at my classmates, fascinated by their hair... long, straight, flowing. Why wasn't my hair like theirs? Why didn't it dance in the wind, slide down my shoulders? I observed them in minute detail. When a lock of hair fell in front of their faces, they pushed it back with a nonchalant gesture, a shake of the head, or the tip of their fingers behind their ears. Back then, I would have given anything to have what we called "good hair." It wasn't just a question of aesthetics. It was a need to belong, to feel normal, loved, and accepted for who you are. What I felt at the time was a mixture of envy, sadness... and shame. Shame for my frizzy hair, which I found ugly. Ashamed of who I was, simply because I'd never been taught to love my texture, my difference.

Each day, I hoped that perhaps they would tire of their fascination, that they would begin to see past my appearance to who I really was. I hoped they would realize that, despite our different skin colors, we were all just children trying to navigate school, friendships, and growing up. But hope is a fragile thing when you're six years old and feeling utterly alone in a sea of curious, sometimes cruel faces.

These daily encounters planted deeper seeds of rejection and self-consciousness. The confident little girl who had excelled in preschool in Guadeloupe began to question herself, to see herself through their eyes. I started to understand that my appearance—my hair, my skin, my very being—was something that marked me as different in ways that felt insurmountable. The journey of learning to navigate a world where I would always stand out had begun, and it would shape every aspect of how I saw myself for years to come.

CHILDHOOD

From left to right: Guadeloupe; my grandma Man Marcel; me at 6 years old; my sister, my mum, and me in Lyon 1975; my daughter Alicia and me.

MARE TET HEADWRAP

"Tête Chaudière" ceremonial
headwrap/hairstyle

Headwrap with 1 point
My heart is free

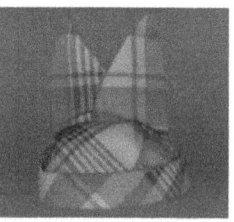

Headwrap with 2 points
My heart is engaged

Headwrap with 3 points
My heart is taken

Headwrap with 4 points
My heart is free

Traditional costume
Guadeloupe-Martinique

Chapter 2: The Pursuit of Conformity

That moment hits you—usually around fifteen or sixteen—when you're standing at the mirror and it all clicks into place: you're wrong. Your body, your face, something. You're looking at a stranger. Someone who doesn't fit.

When I entered middle school, everything changed. I was becoming more aware of my appearance, like any teenage girl trying to figure out where she fits in this world. I was watching television, studying those images like they were textbooks, and what did I see? There were not many Black people on television in France, and the ones who were there—honey, they were wearing only straight hair. Straight, flowing, silky hair that moved when they walked, that caught the light just right.

This became my bible, my standard of beauty. I would sit in front of that television and think, "That's what beautiful looks like. That's what I need to look like."

Do you remember the moment you first encountered something that felt like it could change everything? For me, that moment was discovering relaxer. I thought I had found a miracle. I still remember trying the curly perm (the Jheri curl) after wearing relaxer for a while, but when I first experienced relaxer—ooh la la, what a revelation! I jumped into it as if it were the answer to all my prayers. I was overjoyed. Finally, I could have straight hair, just like the women I admired on television.

I was so determined, so desperate to have that straight hair, that I did this all by myself. Picture this: a teenage girl who couldn't afford to go to a hairdresser, walking around Lyon looking for someone, anyone, who could sell her the key to transformation. And I found him—this one guy, I think he was from Africa, who was selling Black hair products. He had a little boutique at the train station, and when I discovered this place, oh my God, I went there straight away.

I bought that perm box as if it were made of gold. I held it in my hands, reading every word on the package, imagining how I would look. I thought I was going to look like the lady on the box—a beautiful Black woman with straight hair.

For me, it was a rite of passage to adulthood. I went home and did everything myself—mixing the chemicals, applying them to my hair, praying that I wouldn't mess it up. Can you imagine? A teenager playing chemist with her own hair because she wanted so badly to be beautiful. A moment both dreaded and hoped for. Before starting, I read the instructions on the box. I coated my face, ears, and neck with a thick layer of Vaseline to prevent burns and put on gloves. Not for style, no. To protect myself from this toxic, powerful, and dangerous chemical.

The relaxer cream was white and thick, like a paste. Following the instructions, in front of my mirror I applied the relaxer to strand after strand, pulling well on each section. Everything must be smooth and flat. The instructions said to wait twenty minutes before rinsing it out, but after five minutes, I could already feel a tingling sensation on my scalp. Then there was the burning, as if my skull was on fire. Every minute was torture. But I stood still, afraid that if I rinsed too soon, my hair wouldn't be smooth enough, so I gritted my teeth and endured the pain. I wanted this to work. I wanted to be beautiful. I was convinced that I had to tolerate some suffering to be beautiful. Finally, after what seemed like an eternity, it was time to rinse. My scalp was on fire. That's when I saw it. My kinky hair was now straight; it was rippled and longer than usual! Just as I'd always dreamed. I touched it, smiled, and felt a sense of pride. Little did I know that on that day, I had also begun to distance myself from myself. I was on the journey of denying part of my identity for the next 35 years.

My straight hair made me feel so beautiful. I had the same hairstyle as one of my favorite music artists. Sade was my idol; I absolutely loved her. A mixed-race Nigerian-British performer who topped the charts in the 1980s and 1990s, she fronted an all-male band and captivated audiences with her sultry voice and minimalist style. Her signature look was simple yet striking, often just pulling her long hair back into a ponytail and performing on stage barefoot. Have you ever had someone you looked at and thought, "That's exactly who I want to be"? That was Sade for me. I wanted to look like her because she had a prominent forehead like mine, and I just thought she was perfection walking on earth. I always had my hair done, always flat and straight, trying to capture even a hint of that elegance.

That became my routine, my ritual. When I was in school, every three months, like clockwork, I had to retouch. I was trying every product I could find for maintenance, experimenting with every style I could afford. It was constant work, but I didn't care. You know why? Because for the first time in my life, I felt like I belonged somewhere. I felt beautiful. But let me tell you something—this beauty came with a price that wasn't just money.

I soon grew tired of the constant upkeep of retouching my hair with more perm every four to six weeks and wanted a change. Then came the weaves, and oh boy, that was when I really thought I had found the secret to everything. In Paris, they were talking about weaves, and I was so curious, so hungry for this new possibility. I thought, oh mon dieu, I need to do that! My hair was flat, but I wanted extensions that would give me big, long, fluffy hair, allowing me to style it any way I wanted.

I made that trip to Paris by train for my haircare needs. I wanted to find a hairdresser who could do weaves. At the exit of Château d'Eau station, the people commissioned to beckon you into the salons were already closing in on the passengers getting off the train with cards raised, voices insistent—pushing me toward "their" salon, "their" bundles, "their" products.

I let myself be pulled along by the most persistent one. I had never seen so many Black people gathered in one place in France; in Lyon, we were few and scattered. The salon I found myself in felt more like a narrow corridor, dim and crowded, with chairs pressed together and hairdressers working intently over heads in transformation—braiding, relaxing, remaking. The floor was scattered with threads and chopped extensions. A few eyes lifted to meet mine, then the murmur returned. Outside, it was cold; inside, a heavy heat thick with the smell of shea butter, relaxer, and a waft of mafé from a client eating on the spot.

My stylist asked what style I wanted. I said a weave, while holding up two packs of hair I'd bought two streets away. She named a price, and of course, I bargained it down; here, everything was negotiable. She tied a cape around my shoulders and drew neat furrows on my scalp with a fine-toothed comb; I regretted not buying my own, as I had doubts about how clean this one was. Her cornrows lined up like a field of wheat.

She handed me the thick black thread and the needles to thread; I complied, surprised to be "working" as a client. The curved needle slid, sure and steady, anchoring the additions to the braided base, stitch by stitch, invisible yet essential. "Tight, very tight—it has to hold," she said, pulling. My eyes narrowed under the tension; I clenched my teeth. My scalp was on fire, but it was a different kind of pain than the one I felt when applying the relaxer. "It'll pass," she murmured. Between grimaces, I watched her, and I saw pronounced traction alopecia along her frontal hairline; I told myself, if she keeps doing it like this, I'm going to end up with hair ripped from the root and half bald. In the mirror, band after band, the hairstyle took shape.

This marked the beginning of my love affair with my hair. I paid her my hard-earned money, but I did something while she was doing my hair that probably annoyed her to no end. I tracked every move, every angle of the needle, so that I could reproduce this technique with my own hands. I was studying every movement. I was touching the hair, learning with my hands, because I knew I couldn't afford to keep coming back to Paris every time I wanted my hair done. After all, I was a student at the time.

She didn't like me touching, but baby, I didn't care. I was on a mission. I wanted to learn because I didn't want to keep paying those expensive salon prices. And you know what happened? Once I started putting in my own weave, I became good at it. Really good.

This is where my entrepreneurial spirit kicked in. I started doing weaves for people, for money. I was doing braids too—cornrows, box braids, whatever people wanted. I did hair for friends, my mom, and even my mom's friends. I was doing braids for my cousin, for neighbors, for anyone who would trust me with their hair.

Picture this: a teenage Black girl in Lyon, France, running a hair business out of her home. I would either have people come to my house or go to theirs with my little bag of supplies. One woman would tell her friend, and they would book me. Word of mouth, you know? I had to do what I had to do because I didn't have a lot of money, but I wanted my own money so I could do my own things. And let me tell you, there's something powerful about making your own money as a teenager. Every franc I earned doing hair was a form of freedom. It was independence. It was proof that I could take care of myself.

Let me take you back to where this all really began. Let me tell you about my very first experience with straightened hair, because this story will break your heart and make you understand why a nine-year-old girl was conditioned to endure pain for beauty.

It took my first Communion when I was nine years old. Now, if you didn't grow up Catholic like I did, let me explain. In our tradition, after you do Bible study for a certain number of years, you have this ceremony—it's like getting your belt in judo, you know? You have steps, and the first Communion is when you're finally allowed to take the host, the little flat white biscuit with no taste that they give you at church. Many call it Communion, and it's a big deal. It's supposed to be one of the most important events of your young life when you do it for the first time.

My mama bought me a beautiful white dress—I felt like a little princess. But then came the hair. She was going to straighten my hair with a hot comb for this special day. This was my first time having my hair straightened—not with a relaxer, but with a comb heated on the stove until it was smoking hot.

I can still remember sitting in that chair, trying to be still while she worked. And then it happened—she burned my ear. The hot comb touched my ear, and I was smelling the flesh, the burn of my own skin. The pain was incredible, and I said, "Memene, you're burning my head." And she said, "Stop moving." So I stopped moving. I sat there and let her burn me because I wanted beautiful hair for my first Communion.

That burn is deep in my memory, as if I can still feel it to this day. But I was happy because I had straight hair. It wasn't very long, but at least the hot comb stretched it a little bit, and I could feel that it was very smooth and flat. She put big rollers in it to give me little waves for the ceremony, and I felt like I was floating on air.

Every time we had a big event after that—a wedding, a ceremony, whatever—I was getting my hair hot-combed even though that was terrifying for me. I didn't like the hot comb at all. The smell, the fear of being burned again, the way I had to sit perfectly still while this torture happened. But you know what? I did it anyway. Because straight hair meant I was beautiful. Straight hair meant I was worthy of the special occasions.

When I discovered the relaxer as a teenager, it was freedom! No more hot comb, no more burns, no more sitting in fear. I could relax my hair, and it would stay straight for a long time. I didn't think it was a bad thing. Never ever. How could something that made me feel so beautiful be bad?

You need to understand something about me during this time. I had three phases with my hair, each a completely different relationship with what grew out of my head. First was rejection, when I looked in the mirror and saw something that didn't match what the world told me was beautiful. Then came this phase of happiness and love, which was actually a phase of conformity. I loved my hair at that time because finally, I could do whatever I wanted with it and I felt pretty. I felt at peace with myself, like I had solved the puzzle of how to be beautiful. And later, the reality of what those chemicals and weaves were doing to me before accepting my authentic self.

And let me tell you—with the straight hair and weaves, the boys were giving me attention! Oh yes they were! The French boys were looking at me and saying, "Guylaine, you're so beautiful." And that made me feel even prettier, even more confident. When you're a teenager and boys are telling you you're beautiful, you think you've won the lottery. You think you've figured out the secret of life.

But do you know what the real tragedy was? I never questioned why I needed to burn my skin, why I needed to put chemicals in my hair, or why I needed to sew synthetic hair or someone else's hair in, or why I needed to spend so much money, time, and energy just to feel worthy of being seen. I never asked myself, "Why isn't what God gave me good enough?" I just accepted that this was what I had to do to be beautiful. This was the price of admission to the world of pretty girls.

The television was feeding me this idea of beauty, and I was eating it up like I was starving. We had artists like the Caribbean band La Compagnie Créole, with Clemence as the lead singer. Clemence wore beautiful wigs and extensions. And I also loved the American artist Donna Summer—oh, how I adored Donna Summer! Other American artists from the 1980s and '90s that I admired were Tina Turner, Diana Ross, and Whitney Houston. All of these women were icons and wore a variety of wigs, extensions, and weave styles. I really enjoyed watching these artists, who had long, silky hair that flowed like water, as well as a variety of other styles. The few times Black celebrities were shown on television, they were often wearing wigs, but we didn't notice that detail at the time. We just saw the result and thought, "That's what I need to look like."

Even the male artists had their hair coiffed. The American soul singer James Brown had his hair processed, slicked back and perfect. He wore it like that his entire life. When Michael Jackson introduced the Jheri curl, many Black people wanted one too. That style began to gain popularity in the Caribbean and Europe after Michael was seen sporting it.

The one French group that meant everything to us was La Compagnie Créole, as I mentioned. They were playing Creole music, and they were from Guadeloupe and Martinique, like family to us. They were the only Black people we saw on French television who were singing and representing us. Seeing their lead singer wear wigs, our own people began to embrace the notion that straight hair was the way to go, or so we thought.

The only person I really saw with natural hair on television was Bob Marley, but at that time, women didn't typically wear locs, so it didn't resonate with me. Black men wearing an afro or locs during a time when their hair was either processed or short was a revolutionary statement. I saw it in my own family when my uncle started wearing his hair in a huge afro. He was a fan of the Black Panthers, walking around with his fist in the air and his hair like a crown. The teens and adults of the 1970s wore afros, making a statement about how proud they were of their African American culture and roots. You started seeing more of that style after the assassination of Martin Luther King, Jr., as Black Americans moved more into a liberation movement and mindset versus integration. But, for those of us outside the United States, we mostly kept our hair straightened or wore wigs.

In the '70s, my mother used to straighten her hair with a hot iron. She put her hair in tight curlers and sometimes wore wigs, and I'd borrow them on the sly. I'd slip in front of the mirror with my long fake hair and dance and sing like a TV star. But eventually, she too had given in to the trend. She succumbed to the temptation and promise of ease that a perm offered. We termed it "cold straightening." It was the lure of simplicity, modernity, and beauty. A chemical revolution at your fingertips. She was caught between two worlds, just like all of us, because she still loved wearing her wigs as well.

But by the '80s, that liberation and revolution era was winding down. It was more wigs and relaxing. Everybody was relaxing their hair, and if you weren't, people looked at you like something was wrong with you. Like you didn't get the memo about how to be beautiful. Wearing an afro then was a sign that you were not up to the latest hairstyles or that you were unkempt.

My mother never complained about my relaxing my hair. She never said it was bad. How could she? She was doing the same thing to her own hair. She was caught in the same trap, the same cycle of believing that what grew out of our heads wasn't good enough. And my sister? She was completely different from me. She was the tomboy, always into sports, always jogging, wearing workout clothes like she didn't have time for all this beauty nonsense.

She was studying to become a gym teacher, so she didn't care about hair like I did. I was the girly one, the one who spent hours in front of the mirror, the one who believed that beauty was the most important thing a girl could have. We were two sides of the same coin—she rejected all of it, and I embraced all of it. But neither of us questioned why we had to make a choice.

During this time, more Black people were coming to Lyon, but we were still a small community. Most were like my mom—people from the DOM-TOM working in hospitals, post offices, and government jobs. We were the respectable ones, the ones who had made it to mainland France. When we wanted to see a real Black community, we had to travel to Paris, which was approximately five or six hours away by car, around 500 kilometers. For us, going to Paris was like going to another world, you know? It was a city with a growing Black population, which excited me.

I wanted to fit in and belong. I was trying to be beautiful in a world that told me I wasn't enough as I was. This was my phase of love and happiness with my hair—or so I thought. I felt confident, I felt accepted, and I was making money doing hair for others. I never questioned whether it was right or wrong to straighten my hair. It was just what we did. It was normal. It was the price of being a Black woman who was conditioned to believe that European beauty standards were what all women should aspire to attain to feel loved and accepted.

But you know what I realize now? I was living a lie. I was so busy trying to be beautiful according to someone else's standards that I never stopped to ask myself what I thought was beautiful. I never looked in the mirror and asked, "Guylaine, what do you think? What makes you feel like yourself?"

Because the truth was, I didn't know who I was without straight hair. I had been changing myself for so long that I had forgotten what I looked like, what I felt like, who I was when I wasn't trying to be someone else.

Little did I know that this pursuit of conformity would later lead me to question everything I thought I knew about beauty, about myself, and about what it truly meant to be beautiful in my own skin. But that awakening was still years away. For now, I was just a happy teenager with straight hair, walking through the world thinking I had finally figured out how to be beautiful.

I was so wrong. But sometimes, you have to be wrong for a long time before you can be right.

Reflection Questions:

1. What was your first memory of feeling like you needed to change something about your appearance to be considered beautiful?
2. Who were your beauty idols growing up, and how did they shape your understanding of what it meant to be attractive?

Chapter 3: Finding My Voice

There's truth to the saying that home is where the heart is. But sometimes you have to leave to really understand what that means, to see what you had clearly only after it's gone.

My high school years were pretty typical for a teenager. I enjoyed music, dancing, hanging out with friends, and most of all looking pretty and pampering myself. My hair was at the center of it all because I believed that if my hair wasn't looking good, I wasn't completely put together. Sound familiar?

I finally came across Black American magazines like *Essence* and *Ebony* when I moved to London later on. Let me tell you, it was lovely to see beautiful Black women with diverse hairstyles! American women set so many trends.

By the time I was eighteen, I was ready to see the world. I packed my things up and headed over to London to move in with a friend. I attended Kilburn Polytechnic, a graduate school in Northwest London, where I studied and learned English. To make a living, I'd do jobs like waitressing. I intermingled with the Black expats there. We were from Africa and the Caribbean, and it was so nice to be around my people.

Although we were from different parts of the world, our roots were African. I saw Black excellence and ingenuity in them. We were all dealing with different forms of racism and bonded over what we had in common. Our music and food had so much in common. I even see that today as a naturalized American. The African American community shares similar traits with those in the Caribbean and Africa. Our culture runs deep.

Every weekend, I'd immerse myself in the Caribbean scene in London. The parties, barbeques, and gatherings were so much fun. Although we lived in a nation that had historically been one of the biggest colonizers, we created our own space of joy and love. What we had in common was that all Black women had hairstyles that were far removed from our natural texture. We were proud to be Black, but we wanted to fit into the dominant society. Can you relate to that internal conflict?

After two years, I traveled back to France for a few months, trying to figure out my next move. But something deep inside me was calling me home—to my roots, to Guadeloupe. I was ready to leave the cold, damp weather of London and get back to my beautiful country of year-round sunshine and beaches. More than that, I needed to reconnect with my culture, my community, my people.

When I returned to Guadeloupe, I was determined to find work. Picture this: I had a resume in hand and took buses around the island, knocking on the doors of companies in the economic center, letting them know I was looking for a job. I was persistent and fearless in my approach. You know what? It worked! Eventually, I landed a secretary position at a marketing company. It felt good to be working again, contributing, and building something.

But workplace dynamics—they were complicated. Some of the other women seemed hostile towards me, perhaps because I had traveled and experienced different cultures, or maybe because of the attention I received. I had lived my life in France, so my accent and style were different than most in Guadeloupe. I felt like a stranger in my own country. It was a reminder that even among our own people, there could be competition and envy. Have you ever experienced that? It's heartbreaking when it happens.

What struck me most about being back in Guadeloupe was how universal the hair straighteners were, especially in the tourist industry where I worked. Everyone—and I mean everyone—had straightened hair. This was in the mid-1990s, and there was no significant natural hair movement at the time.

I remember it being said that these women with natural hair belonged to certain religious communities, notably the Adventist Church, but also to the nascent Rasta movement that developed in Guadeloupe in the 1980s and 1990s. Their beauty was unadorned: no makeup, no artifice; just the raw, rich texture of their hair, a testament to an allegiance to a faith or ideology that valued the "natural." In my youthful judgment, they seemed unrefined. But I was sorely mistaken. These women were beautiful.

Some Black men in Guadeloupe preferred women with straight hair. Men's perceptions mattered: women with fair skin and straight or slightly wavy hair, often the product of complex mixed races, were celebrated in Caribbean societies. The mixture of European, Indian, or African origins was designated by terms rooted in colonial history—Mulatto, Chabine, Chappe-cooli, or Battazyndien—each classifying specific nuances of mixed races and hair textures. They embodied a socially valued ideal of beauty.

These categories allowed for a subtle hierarchy of physical traits: fair skin, "beautiful" hair (wavy rather than kinky), a thinner nose, all indicators of European or Indian ancestry, considered aesthetically privileged. On the other hand, women with kinky hair and darker skin were often forced to resort to artificial techniques, like hair straightening, in order to approximate this model and please others.

Straight hair became a symbol of elitism, representing a closer connection to European culture. Black women would straighten their hair to appear more like these women, to fit into what society deemed beautiful and acceptable. Isn't it wild how deeply these colonial influences shaped what we consider beautiful?

Now that I was in my "love phase" with my hair, or so I thought, I was getting more attention from men in Guadeloupe, and my hair was a big part of that. I experimented with different styles, extensions, and treatments. Yet despite all this attention, I was still critical of myself. I was envious of women with naturally long, straight hair. I saw my own hair as something that needed to be constantly managed, controlled, and altered to be acceptable.

In the corporate world, you had to stick to the "corporate look." Your hair had to be neat, straight, and professional. There was no room for creativity or natural texture. It was just expected, and I followed along without question because that's what successful women did. We all have those unspoken rules we follow, don't we?

Despite the hair pressures, I enjoyed my life back in Guadeloupe. I was surrounded by friends and family again, speaking my language, eating my food, feeling the warmth of my culture. At 24, I got married to the father of my first son. The marriage lasted two years—sometimes life takes you in directions you don't expect, and that's okay. We do what we need to do to grow and learn.

Then something amazing happened that changed everything. I landed a job on television as a weather reporter. This marked the beginning of a 25-year career in media. Initially, I was just reporting the weather, but television opened up a whole new world for me. I discovered that I had a natural talent for being on camera, connecting with people, and communicating in a way that resonated with audiences.

The television industry was interesting when it came to hair. Unlike the rigid corporate world, television actually encouraged a bit more variety in hairstyles, but I still had to be conservative. Each week, I would visit a hairdresser for free because the salon would offer me complimentary services—and it was a lot of fun! The public loved to see what new hairstyle I would have. I became known for my beautiful hair, and people would tune in partly to see what I was doing with my hair that week. Can you imagine? My hair became part of my brand for private television in Guadeloupe, L'A1!

I eventually transitioned from weather reporting to hosting my own shows on the RFO regional Channel of France. I created two main programs: *Midi Service*, where I offered advice and invited professional guests, and *Conviction Intime*, a talk show that explored social issues, sexuality, mental health, and even gave a platform to people living with illnesses like AIDS. For its time, the show was groundbreaking. I loved pushing boundaries and sparking conversations that others were hesitant to have.

Of all my media work over 25 years, radio was what I enjoyed most. I hosted a two-hour live show every day, and the connection with my audience meant everything to me. I loved them, and they loved me back. The 7,000 listeners who tuned in each morning felt like family and friends. Radio gave me a sense of comfort, because appearance didn't matter—it was just about voice and connection. Alongside my radio work for the French branch of National Television, I also hosted a television program with them.

I loved pushing boundaries, challenging people to think differently, and creating spaces for important conversations that weren't happening elsewhere. It felt like I was finally using my voice for something meaningful.

My hair journey during this time was fascinating. I was still very much in my love phase, constantly changing styles, experimenting with different looks. The freedom that television gave me with my hair was liberating in some ways, but I was still operating within the framework of straight, processed hair. I wasn't questioning the fundamental assumption that my natural hair wasn't good enough —I was just finding more creative ways to style the hair that I had altered. I loved the styles I could create, the attention I received, and the versatility I had—but I wasn't loving my actual hair. I was loving what I could make it become.

The acceptance phase was still years away. That would come much later, when I would finally embrace my natural texture and understand that my hair was beautiful exactly as it grew from my scalp. But during my time in Guadeloupe, and in my television career, when I was in love, I was content with the creative expression I had found, even if it wasn't authentic to my natural self.

My 25 years in media, spanning both radio and television, were formative. They taught me how to communicate, how to connect with people, and how to address difficult topics with grace and courage. They also taught me about the power of image, about how appearance affects how people perceive and receive your message.

But perhaps most importantly, they taught me that I had a voice. That I could use that voice to create change, to challenge norms, to help people think differently about important issues. Even if I hadn't yet found my authentic voice when it came to my own hair, I was learning to use my voice to help others find theirs.

Reflection Questions

1. **Your Own Beauty Standards**: What beauty standards from your culture or community have you internalized without questioning? How might these standards be limiting your authentic self-expression?
2. **Love vs. Acceptance**: Is there something about yourself that you think you love, but you're actually only loving when it's modified or changed? What would true acceptance look like for you?

HAIR STYLES IN MY MEDIA ERA

From 1996 to 2018

Chapter 4: Facing the Mirror Publicly

You know that moment when you're standing at a crossroads and you can feel your whole life about to change? That's exactly where I found myself in 2015. I had been on television for years, switching up my hairstyles weekly, being creative with extensions and weaves, loving the attention and the freedom to experiment. But something was shifting inside me, something I couldn't ignore anymore.

Picture this: every week, I would sit in that salon chair, having my hair transformed into yet another style. The viewers loved it—they would tune in partly just to see what Guylaine was going to do with her hair this time. My different hairstyles on television made me recognizable and beloved. The salon visits were free because I partnered with them in exchange for increased visibility, and the styles were creative and beautiful. I felt like I had found the perfect balance between professionalism and self-expression.

But beneath all that glamour, my body was screaming at me to stop.

The chemicals were taking their toll in ways I could no longer ignore. My scalp was constantly irritated, burning and itching after every relaxer treatment. My hairline was receding, creating gaps that I had to cover with strategic styling. The extensions were pulling at my natural hair, creating tension headaches that would last for days. I spent hours in that salon chair getting my hair sewn into my head or relaxed and styled, but deep down, I knew it wasn't really the authentic me.

The worst part? I was trapped in a cycle. The more damaged my natural hair became from the chemicals and manipulation, the more I felt I needed the extensions and treatments to cover up the damage. It was like being addicted to something that was slowly poisoning me, but feeling like I couldn't function without it.

But here's the thing that made my situation even more complicated —I wasn't just making a personal choice in the privacy of my bedroom. I was on the radio and television. Whatever I did, an entire island would see, and they would know. Every choice I made about my appearance would be scrutinized, discussed, and judged by thousands of viewers. The pressure was immense.

Let me paint you a picture of what Guadeloupe was like in 2015 when it came to natural hair. There were NO examples of Black women on television with natural hair. None. Zero. I would have been one of the first television hosts to appear on screen with my natural texture if I had decided to take that route. Can you imagine the pressure? The fear?

In our media landscape, the expectation was crystal clear. If you wanted to be taken seriously as a professional and seen as beautiful and polished, you had straight hair. Period. It wasn't even a conversation or a choice—it was just the way things were. The Black women who appeared on television all had the same look: straightened, styled, and controlled hair that conformed to European beauty standards.

I remember lying awake at night, touching my scalp where it was tender from the last relaxer, wondering how much longer I could keep this up. The breaking point came when I visited a dermatologist to help my hair grow back. I'd started injections and pills for it, and I realized that continuing with what I was calling "this crazy chemical stuff" wasn't making any sense anymore. The irritation was spreading, and I was developing what felt like allergic reactions to products I'd been using for years.

But I want to be completely honest with you—I didn't make this decision to go natural from a place of pride or empowerment. I wasn't ready to say, "Hey, I'm proud! Look at me with my natural hair!" It wasn't some beautiful moment of self-acceptance and Black power. It was purely a health decision. I was rejecting the chemicals because they were literally making me sick, but I wasn't yet embracing my natural hair with love and acceptance. That would come later, much later.

The day I decided to cut off all my chemically processed hair was one of the scariest days of my life. I sat in that salon chair—the same chair where I'd had so many beautiful styles created—and watched years of processed hair fall to the floor. So many thoughts were running through my mind, mainly whether or not I'd look presentable. What was left was short, natural, and completely foreign to me. I had been hiding my natural texture for so long that I barely recognized it.

I remember my colleague took a picture of me right after the cut— and, honey, I didn't even want to see that picture! The rejection I felt toward my own image was real and painful. I looked at myself and felt... disappointed. Scared. Like I had just made a terrible mistake. I had the same feeling as I did as a little girl, with short hair, before moving to France.

But there was no going back. I had made the decision, and in a few days, I would have to appear on television with this new look. I spent those days trying to figure out how to style my short natural hair, how to make it look "presentable" for television, and how to minimize the shock for my viewers.

The night before my first appearance with natural hair, I couldn't sleep. I kept thinking about all the things that could go wrong. And all the potential negative feedback. If I didn't like myself, how could they? But let me tell you what happened when I stepped in front of those cameras with my natural hair: the response was immediate and powerful, but not in the way I expected. The crew was professional, as always, but I could feel their curiosity. Some seemed genuinely impressed by my courage, and others looked uncertain about how the viewers would receive this. But the cameras rolled, and I delivered my show with the same energy and professionalism I always brought.

The reaction from viewers started almost immediately. The phone lines lit up. Social media exploded. People in restaurants would recognize me, but now they were also asking about my hair. They were asking me things like, "What made you decide to do this?" "It looks ok, I think we will get used to it." "Do you like it better than your old hair?"

Women were whispering to each other when they saw me. Some would approach me saying things like, "I've been thinking about going natural, but I was too scared. Seeing you on TV makes me feel like maybe I can do it too."

But not all the reactions were positive. Even my mum asked if I was going to comb my hair to appear on television because I didn't look professional. Some viewers were confused, even critical. I received comments questioning my choice, asking why I would "let myself go" or "lower my standards." Some people felt I looked less professional, less polished than before, with a "neglected hairstyle."

It took me a few months to start accepting what I saw in the mirror. A few months to stop feeling like I was compromising my appearance for my health and start seeing the beauty in my natural texture. Every morning, I would look at myself and feel a mix of emotions—sometimes pride for my courage, sometimes regret for what I'd lost, sometimes confusion about who this new person in the mirror was.

I had to learn how to style my natural hair for television. This wasn't just about personal acceptance—I had to figure out how to make my hair look polished and professional in front of cameras and lights. I experimented with different products, techniques, and styles. Some days were better than others. Some days, I felt beautiful and confident; other days, I missed the ease and versatility of my extensions.

But you know what really opened my eyes? What shifted everything for me? My daughter. She was in pre-K at the time, and because I lived in a very touristy area of Guadeloupe, Le Gosier, there was a huge European population at her school. The demographics of her classroom reflected the international nature of our community—French children, Dominican, Haitian, expat kids, and children of tourists who were staying for extended periods.

One day, my daughter came home from school, and I could tell something was bothering her. She looked up at me with those big, serious eyes that children get when they're trying to process something complicated. "Mommy," she said, "I don't like my hair. I want my hair to look like my friend Lea." My heart stopped. Lea was her best friend at school—a sweet little girl with blue eyes and long, straight blonde hair. The physical traits that white society had taught us were the epitome of beauty. "Why don't you like your hair, baby?" I asked, trying to keep my voice calm even though I was sad inside because I realized I wasn't a good example for her. "It's not pretty like Lea's," she said matter-of-factly. "Hers is long and soft and pretty. Mine is... different—ugly."

For her entire little life, she had only seen me with straight hair or curly extensions. Every photo on our walls, every memory she had of me getting ready for work, every time she'd watched me on television, I had been wearing extensions or relaxed hair. I had never given her an example of natural hair being beautiful. I had never shown her that she was gorgeous exactly as she was.

That moment changed everything for me. This wasn't just about my health anymore, or my career image, or my personal journey with self-acceptance. This was about the message I was sending to my daughter about what was beautiful, what was acceptable, and what was worthy of love and admiration.

How could I tell this precious little girl that she was beautiful with her natural hair if I wasn't showing her that with my own? How could I teach her to love herself authentically if I were still struggling to love myself? How could I be the example she needed if I were hiding my true self from the world?

That night, I sat down with my daughter and did something my mother never did with me. I spoke with her about her beautiful natural hair. I told her she was gorgeous exactly as she was. I showed her pictures of beautiful Black women with natural hair—models, actresses, everyday women who were rocking their natural texture with confidence and pride. I had to show her that her hair was beautiful. "It's alive and strong and uniquely yours. Lea's hair is beautiful too, but different doesn't mean better or worse. It just means something different," I explained.

We looked at pictures together, and slowly, I started believing it about myself too. As I was teaching my daughter to love her natural hair, I was learning to love mine. We were on this journey of acceptance together, mother and daughter, figuring out how to see beauty in what we'd been taught to hide.

I would braid her hair, sometimes adding extensions. These sessions took place on Sunday afternoons to prepare her for the week ahead. After washing her hair and gently detangling it, we would settle down for our ritual. She would sit on a cushion between my legs. Styling her hair was never a simple routine; it was a sacred gesture passed down through the ages. I carefully parted her hair—parting is an art in itself—and braided it into neat plaits, always taking care not to pull too hard, aware of the risk of alopecia associated with tension. Yet even with my gentlest touch, she would grimace and grumble. But we both knew that this was our moment of connection, my hands in her hair, bound by lineage, just as our mothers and grandmothers had been before us.

You have to understand the historical context of what we were doing. In the postcolonial French West Indies (Guadeloupe, Martinique, and Guyane), the legacy of colonization continues to shape perceptions of beauty, identity, and belonging. As Josépha Labbé points out in her critical exploration of Caribbean aesthetics, colonial powers did not merely control land and bodies; they also imposed cultural hierarchies that favored European traits, values, and norms. The natural hair of Guadeloupeans of African descent, once a symbol of ancestral pride and resistance, was stigmatized under colonial rule. Straightened hair, light skin, and European clothing were encouraged as signs of respectability and social advancement, while curly hair was equated with savagery, disorder, or lack of civility. This internalized racism has left a lasting psychological mark, which today manifests itself in both shame and the assertion of natural hair. Labbé's work highlights how these imposed standards continue to influence everyday choices and social pressures, making the act of wearing natural hair not only personal but also political.

For generations, Black women in Guadeloupe straightened their hair to conform to what society deemed beautiful and acceptable. Going natural on television wasn't just a personal choice—it was a challenge to hundreds of years of internalized colonialism. It was a political statement, whether I intended it to be or not.

We were also heavily influenced by American culture and Caribbean trends. We watched American TV shows, listened to American music, and followed American fashion. During this time, the natural hair movement was gaining momentum in the United States, with celebrities like Solange Knowles and Issa Rae embracing their natural textures. But even with these positive examples, the dominant images in the media were still of straight, processed hair.

In Caribbean culture, including that of Guadeloupe, we were also influenced by Jamaica, where locs held cultural and spiritual significance. But even there, natural hair was often associated with Rastafarianism or counterculture movements. It wasn't seen as mainstream or professional. People wearing locs were considered drug dealers or bad boys.

After I went natural, something beautiful started happening that I never expected. Other women began reaching out to me—not just viewers, but women in the media industry itself. A colleague, Christelle, who was a journalist on television, sent me a message that I'll never forget: "Thank you, because I was thinking about presenting the news with my natural hair. Seeing you gave me the courage to go natural too." She has now been wearing her natural hair on television for over 10 years, and it has never been an issue for her career. But she needed to see someone else do it first. She needed to see that it was possible to be professional, successful, and authentically herself.

I had become one of the pioneers without meaning to. That opened doors for other women to see that it was possible. I had given them permission to be themselves. But let me be real with you—this journey wasn't all sunshine and empowerment. There were real consequences to being different, to standing out, to challenging the status quo.

But even though it was a challenging period, I didn't regret my choice. My hair was healthier than it had been in years. My scalp was healing. And I was learning that sometimes the right choices come with difficult consequences, but that doesn't make them wrong choices.

My children's reactions to my natural hair journey were interesting. My oldest son, who was an adult by then, had flown to the UK to pursue his dance career. He had locs. I didn't like his hairstyle because of the reputation of people with locs, and I was scared it would hold his career back. All three of my children were fine with my new look and style. They had grown accustomed to me wearing my hair in different ways, so going natural was no big deal to them. In their eyes, I was still Mom and not just a lady on television.

My intimate life became its own kind of performance. None of my partners had ever seen my real hair, not once. When it came to closeness, I had to become a magician, constantly inventing ways to create distance while appearing present. The secret sat between us like something unspeakable: I was wearing someone else's hair.

The possibility that they might figure it out terrified me. Not just figure it out, but *know* it. That shame lived in my chest, heavy and constant.

But there was something else, something I rarely admitted even to myself. No matter how many times I washed those synthetic strands, or how carefully I maintained them, they carried a smell. Not pleasant. A complicated mixture of sweat, product buildup, and the mustiness that comes from moisture trapped beneath something that isn't meant to breathe. If someone leaned in close enough during a tender moment, if they really got close, they would catch the scent.

So I developed a careful choreography of my own body. Certain spaces became off-limits. A no-touch zone during our most vulnerable moments together. I held them at a distance even when I was holding them, protecting a secret I couldn't bear to share.

What I didn't realize at the time was how common this was. Later on, sitting with Black women friends back in the United States, I began to hear their stories. They had the same careful distance regarding intimacy, and the same shame. For so many of us, wigs and extensions weren't just about hair. In those intimate moments, they became symbols of something deeper—a weight we carried, even when we were most vulnerable, as if vulnerability itself wasn't enough. As if, no matter how close we let someone get, there was always this one place we had to hide.

Hair had always been a loaded topic at work—whether long or short, natural or enhanced, it meant far more than style. In the radio and TV corridors, colleagues often complimented one another, and whenever someone chose to go natural, it felt like a small celebration: you're one of us, you belong. I still visited Nadine, my trusted stylist, to add kinky extensions now and then—just to revel in the full, voluminous glory of a big Afro. On weeks when time slipped away, I reached for my backup: an Afro wig. It wasn't only about convenience; it was about holding on to a version of myself that felt bold, free, and familiar in a world that often asked me to be something else.

By the mid-2010s, more Black men started growing locs more openly, even though it had previously been seen as something only "bad boys" or gang members did. Professional men began wearing locs to business meetings, challenging the idea that natural hair was unprofessional or inappropriate for corporate settings.

The influence wasn't just local, either; from Paris to the rest of Europe, the internet was overflowing with DIY tutorials celebrating natural ("nappy") hair. YouTube channels, forums, and blogs became classrooms where we learned, shared routines, and reclaimed our crowns together. We were all part of this global movement toward authenticity, even though we were dealing with our own unique cultural pressures and historical contexts.

It's fascinating to think about how interconnected these movements were. While I was facing my fears about appearing publicly with natural hair in Guadeloupe, women in Atlanta, Detroit, and Los Angeles were having their own "big chop" moments. We were all part of something bigger than ourselves, all contributing to a shift in how Black women around the world saw themselves and their natural beauty.

But we still have a long way to go, and I want to be honest about that. Even now, with more acceptance of natural hair, we're still bombarded with images that tell us long, straight hair is the standard of beauty. Social media, music videos, movies—they all still predominantly show processed hair and wigs as the ideal.

I think about artists like Beyoncé, whose influence on global beauty standards is undeniable. While she has occasionally embraced natural styles, her signature look has often featured long, straight hair or extensions. This isn't a critique of her choices; rather, it highlights how influential figures can shape perceptions of beauty, and how those images can impact how young women view themselves and define their own standards.

The same is true for social media influencers and celebrities from the Caribbean and other parts of the diaspora. Many of them still rely heavily on wigs, weaves, and extensions to maintain their image. While there's nothing wrong with these choices individually, collectively they reinforce the message that natural hair isn't quite good enough for success or admiration.

But I've also seen incredible progress. Young women today have access to so much more information about caring for their natural hair. There are YouTube channels, Instagram accounts, and entire businesses built around celebrating and supporting natural hair journeys. The options for products, techniques, and styles have exploded in ways I could never have imagined when I first went natural.

Looking back now, I realize that appearing in the media with my natural hair was one of the most important things I have ever done—not just for myself, but for my community and for Black women more broadly. I showed little girls like my daughter that they were beautiful exactly as they were. I proved that success and professionalism weren't tied to conforming to European beauty standards.

There were mornings when I looked in the mirror and missed my long hair. There were days when styling my natural hair felt like a struggle, when I wondered if I had made things unnecessarily difficult for myself. There were moments when I questioned whether the health benefits were worth the professional and social challenges.

But each time I saw my daughter confidently wearing her natural hair to school, each time I received a message from a woman thanking me for inspiring her journey, each time I looked at my healthy scalp and strong hairline, I knew I had made the right choice.

The journey taught me that authenticity isn't a destination, it's a daily choice. Every morning, I had to choose to love what I saw in the mirror. Every time I appeared on camera, I had to choose confidence over insecurity. Every time someone questioned my choice, I had to choose to trust my own judgment over their opinions.

That's the thing about facing the mirror publicly—whether it's literal like mine was, or metaphorical in your own life. You can't wait until you feel completely confident and self-assured. Sometimes you have to step into your authenticity scared, unsure, and with your knees shaking. The strength comes from doing it anyway.

Sometimes you have to be willing to be the first, to be different, to risk everything you've built for the chance to be genuinely yourself. And sometimes, just sometimes, that courage opens doors not just for you, but for everyone who comes after you.

Reflection Questions

1. **Health vs. Image**: Have you ever continued habits or practices that were harmful to your physical or mental health because of how others expected you to look or behave? What would it take to prioritize your well-being over others' expectations?
2. **Acting before Feeling Ready**: Think of a time when you had to act authentically before you felt confident about it. What did you learn from stepping into your truth while still feeling uncertain?

Chapter 5: The Awakening

There comes a moment when everything you thought you knew about yourself begins to tremble, when the ground beneath you shifts, revealing that what you believed was solid has been quietly giving way all along.

When I moved to the United States in 2017, I wasn't prepared for what I would encounter. I came to Florida for professional reasons, to study English, and to take a break from the tension and stress of work and a recent divorce. I had to give myself space to breathe. I brought my son with me first, and later my daughter joined us. I thought I was just taking a one-year sabbatical, you know? Just a little pause. But life had other plans for me.

I was walking around Florida with my natural hair, and I still hadn't fully embraced who I was yet. I was still unsatisfied with my image. I still didn't love what I saw in the mirror. But I was wearing my natural hair anyway, trying to make peace with this stranger I saw looking back at me.

One day, I began to notice something that shocked me to my core. The Black women in Florida—OH MON DIEU! They were wearing so many wigs! Especially the ones with baby hair along the hairline, the edges all laid to perfection, as if they were going to a photo shoot every single day. I was surprised because in Guadeloupe and in Paris, wigs were not the trend. More Black women were starting to wear their hair naturally. We didn't have all these elaborate wigs with the perfectly sculpted edges. Yes, natural hair was starting to gain popularity in the United States, but more women still wore weaves and wigs than not.

It was like stepping into a completely different world, a world where Black women had taken the art of hair transformation to a level I had never seen before. These weren't the simple wigs of my youth in France. These were masterpieces: lace fronts that looked as if they had grown right out of their scalps, colored hair that changed weekly, and lengths that went from bob to waist-length overnight. The creativity and artistry in these wigs were something to behold, but they still weren't enough for me to want to wear them and cover up my natural hair.

I remember asking one of my friends one day, "What's going on? You always wear wigs. I never see your natural hair. Don't you ever want to just... let your hair breathe?" She looked at me with this shame in her eyes, the kind of shame I recognized because I had carried it for so many years, and said, "Because I don't like my hair. I hate seeing my real hair. When I look at my natural hair, all I see is... nothing good."

She was just like me, just like the woman I used to be. Just like millions of women who had been taught that what grows out of our heads isn't beautiful enough, isn't professional enough, isn't worthy enough.

That conversation haunted me. Here I was, a woman who had spent decades chemically altering my hair, looking at another woman who was doing the same thing but with different tools. The methods had evolved, but the message remained the same: you are not enough as you are.

That's when something clicked inside me. It was before the COVID pandemic, and I decided to dig a little bit deeper. I started asking questions, not just about hair, but about everything. Why did we all feel this way? Where did this shame come from? How did we get here?

And that's when I picked up a paintbrush for the first time with real intention.

I had always loved art, always felt drawn to creating something beautiful. When I was little, and we visited the Louvre in Paris, I fell in love with the paintings on the walls. The way light played across faces, the way artists could capture not just what someone looked like, but who they were inside. But you know what I never saw in all those museums, in all those galleries, in all those art books? Black women.

Every time I traveled, every museum I visited, every art exhibition I attended, I never saw women who looked like me hanging on those walls. And I loved art so much that this absence hurt my heart. The images of the women I saw in those paintings were all white. None of them looked like me. It was like walking through a world where I didn't exist, where my beauty, my story, my very presence was invisible. So I said to myself, "If I'm ever going to paint, I want to see women like me. I'm going to paint Black women, and I'm going to paint them with their natural hair."

But that decision didn't come easy. I had bought art supplies, but for months, I would sit in front of blank canvases, paintbrush in hand, paralyzed by doubt. Who was I to think I could be an artist? Who was I to think my story mattered? Who was I to think I could create something that would make people feel seen?

The imposter syndrome was real, honey. Really real. I would start painting a face and then stop, convinced I was fooling myself. I would look at other artists' work and think, "You'll never be that good. You're just a journalist pretending to be an artist."

But every time I was about to give up, I would remember that conversation with my friend about her hair. I would remember all the years I spent looking in the mirror and seeing failure staring back at me. I would remember all the Black girls and women who had never seen themselves represented as beautiful, as worthy, as enough.

That's how this whole journey really began, with a paintbrush, a decision to tell my story, and a refusal to let fear win.

I didn't want to paint birds, flowers, or pretty landscapes that would look nice above someone's couch. I wanted to paint for a purpose. I wanted my paintings to mean something, something to me, something to my people, something to anyone who had ever felt invisible in this world. I wanted to tell stories that had never been told, show faces that had never been seen, and celebrate hair that had never been celebrated.

And as I started to draw, really draw, I started to study the hair story. Not just the surface level—not just the "oh, relaxers are bad for you" kind of knowledge—but the deep, historical, political, economic truth about what had been done to us and what we had been convinced to do to ourselves.

As I painted, learned, read, and researched, I finally came to understand the magnitude of what had been done to us, and I started to truly love my hair for the first time in my life. Not just accept it. Not just tolerate it. Not just wear it because it was healthier. I started to love it. I started to love who I was. I started to embrace who I was. Every brushstroke was an act of self-acceptance. Every face I painted with an afro, with braids, with locs, with twist-outs—it was me learning to see beauty in what I had always been taught was ugly.

I am a self-taught artist. I tried to take a few classes, but I didn't like the methods the teachers were instructing me to follow. I choose the medium of oil on canvas, and my style is figurative narrative, because I have a story to tell. Initially, I would paint Black women in black and white because I wanted people to focus on their hair. I didn't want them distracted by colorful clothing or elaborate backgrounds. I wanted them to look directly at these faces, these expressions, these crowns of natural hair, and really see them.

I wanted them to see the hair story, to understand that this isn't just about vanity or personal preference—this is about reclaiming our identity, our history, our right to exist as we are without apology.

Every painting became a prayer, a declaration, a small act of revolution. When I painted a woman with a magnificent afro, I was saying, "This is beautiful." When I painted locs cascading down a woman's shoulders, I was saying, "This is professional." When I painted short natural hair with silver strands, I was saying, "This is worthy."

And you know what happened as I painted these women, spending hours looking at Black faces and natural hair textures, and finding new ways to capture their beauty? Not the version of myself with straight hair that I had spent decades trying to perfect. Not the version that looked like someone else's idea of beautiful. But me. The real me. The me that God made.

That's when I discovered the book that changed my life: *Hair Stories: Untangling the Roots of Black Hair in America*, by Ayana Byrd and Lori Tharps. Oh mon dieu, when I opened that book, when I read the first chapter, when I started to understand the scope of what I had been living through, it was like someone had turned on every light in a house I didn't even know was dark.

I read that book like it was the Bible, like it held the secrets to everything I had never understood about myself. I watched videos on YouTube, read theses on hair stories, watched the Chris Rock documentary film called *Good Hair*, and looked for anything I could find about Black hair, including following social media hashtags like #afrohair. I tried to capture everything I could relate to our hair stories. The more I discovered and learned, the more enlightened I became. I got angry. I felt relieved. I felt vindicated. I felt foolish for not knowing all of this sooner.

That book became my awakening. It was a revelation that shook me to my core. For the first time in my life, I understood why I had spent so many years hating what grew out of my head. I understood that this hatred wasn't natural, wasn't inevitable, wasn't just "the way things are."

I learned about our ancestors and how sacred hair was to them, the spirituality of hair in Africa, before our people were stolen and brought to the Americas and to the Caribbean. I learned about the intricate braiding patterns that served as maps for escaped slaves, as well as how hairstyles indicated social status, marital status, and tribal affiliation. Our hair told stories. Our hair held power.

And then I learned how the colonizers systematically tried to erase our hair identity, just like they tried to erase our culture, our languages, our religions, our very sense of self. They didn't just take our freedom; they took our understanding of our own beauty.

When I read that book, I finally understood the stigmatization of Black hair wasn't accidental. It was intentional. It was strategic and systematic. It was designed to make us believe that everything about us needed to be fixed, changed, improved, and made more palatable to white sensibilities.

I understood that behind hair, it's not just about aesthetics, it's really a question of identity. It's my identity that they tried to erase. My history they tried to rewrite. My sense of self they tried to destroy.

But it's also a question of economics, and this part made me so angry I could barely contain myself. Black women spend billions of dollars every year trying to "fix" our hair. A deliberate economic disparity is built into this system. When you have to buy wigs and relaxers and extensions and all the tools to maintain them, and you're making minimum wage, you're spending sometimes 30% or more of your income on hair products just to be considered acceptable in the workplace.

I've been able to unlearn many negative perceptions about Black hair, thanks to books, videos, papers, and research. We have to spend more money than white women just to be seen as professional, just to get hired, just to keep our jobs. And then we wonder why we can't get ahead financially? We're literally paying for the privilege of conforming to someone else's standard of beauty.

Your hair tells your story—who you are, what you can afford, where you belong. It's politics written on your scalp. It's health. It's power.

I learned about the inventors of relaxers, as well as many manufacturers that built empires on our insecurities. I learned about the whole beauty industry that profits from convincing us that we need to be fixed. I learned how, after slavery, Black people—especially Black women—had to be incredibly ingenious, incredibly strategic, just to survive.

We were forced to conform. We had to straighten our hair to be accepted for jobs, to be seen as respectable, to be allowed into certain spaces. The more we looked like white people, the more access we had to opportunities. It was a survival mechanism that became so internalized we forgot it wasn't our choice—we started believing it was our preference.

This brainwashing had been going on for 400 years! 400 years of systematic psychological warfare designed to make us believe that what grows naturally out of our heads isn't good enough, isn't professional enough, isn't beautiful enough.

And I learned something else that broke my heart and made me furious at the same time—the products we were using to "fix" our hair were literally harming our health. The chemicals in relaxers have been linked to cancer, to reproductive issues, to scalp damage that never heals. I was a victim of the harm it does. It's a vicious circle designed to keep us trapped. We damage our hair and our health trying to be beautiful according to someone else's standards, and then we have to spend more money trying to fix the damage we caused trying to be acceptable.

Thanks to Dr. Melvin Rouse, a neuroendocrinologist, I learned something that changed my understanding of the effects of the chemicals in the hair products I'd been using and what they were doing to my body. I learned that the hair products many of us rely on, such as relaxers, straighteners, leave-in conditioners, and scalp treatments, contain chemicals called endocrine disruptors.

These aren't just sitting on your hair. They get into your body. Your hormones. And over time, they can affect your menstruation, your ability to get pregnant, and your pregnancy itself. They've been linked to fibroids and uterine cancer. The evidence is there: women who use these products have higher levels of phthalates, parabens, and phenols in their urine. What we put on our scalp doesn't stay on our scalp. It enters through our skin, through the air we breathe, through our hands to our mouths, and even through breast milk.

"No lie" marketing is itself a lie.

But here's what really matters: this doesn't affect everyone the same way. Black women face a disproportionate exposure not by accident, but by design. We've been targeted with products containing riskier formulas for decades. We start using them at a younger age and continue to use them longer due to beauty standards and workplace expectations. Nine out of ten Black women have relaxed their hair at some point in their lives.

When I learned about this, I felt something between fury and grief. I have fibroids. All three of my children were born premature. Three for three. After 35 years of using relaxers, I started connecting the dots that so many of my friends had already noticed. With no family history of these issues, I keep asking: Why us? Why are we the ones being exposed to these chemicals? Why don't these boxes come with the same warnings as cigarettes? Why do companies keep choosing to target us with formulas they know are risky?

We deserve real answers. We deserve transparency. We deserve safer products—and we deserve companies and regulators to finally stop treating Black women's health as negotiable.

They made money when we straightened our hair. They made money when our hair fell out. They made money when we bought wigs to cover the damage. They made money when we got sick from the chemicals. At every single step of our journey toward self-destruction, someone was profiting.

I learned about something that Dr. Tammy White-Jolivette calls Post-Traumatic Hair Syndrome (PTHS). It's a term that describes the emotional and psychological weight of hair discrimination, of being told your hair isn't right, of losing it, of being pressured to change it. It happens at work, at school, or in comments from strangers. It's the humiliation of not fitting the unwritten rules about what "professional" or "acceptable" looks like. It's the trauma of watching your hair thin or disappear.

But here's what matters: PTHS® isn't just about vanity. It's not just, "oh, I don't like how I look." It goes deeper than that. It affects who you think you are. It shakes your confidence. It can lead to shame, anxiety, and even grief. It makes you second-guess yourself, avoid situations, and censor who you are.

The good news is that healing is possible. It starts with education, really understanding the psychological toll of hair-related trauma and learning concrete ways to rebuild your sense of self and confidence. Support groups help. Talking to therapists and dermatologists when you need to.

But it can't stop there. Schools need to change their dress codes. Workplaces need to stop policing Black hair. Salons and healthcare providers need cultural competence training. We need institutions that genuinely understand hair inclusion, recognizing it as an equity issue, not a preference issue. We need policies and practices that protect people, support them when harm happens, and help restore their dignity and sense of agency.

I began to see my own reflection in a new light. Those features I had always thought were too wide, too full, too much—suddenly they looked like the faces I was painting with such love and care. That hair I had spent so much money, time, and pain trying to change—suddenly it looked like the crowns I was celebrating on canvas.

That awakening didn't happen overnight. It was a process, like watching the sun rise slowly over the horizon. Some days I would catch a glimpse of self-love and think, "Oh, there it is." On other days, I would slip back into old patterns of criticism and shame.

But gradually, the light grew stronger. The voice in my head that had always been so critical, so harsh, so convinced of my inadequacy, that voice started to quiet down. And in the silence, I could finally hear a different voice. A voice that said, "You are beautiful. You have always been beautiful. You just forgot how to see it."

When that light finally broke through completely, when I finally saw myself clearly for the first time in decades, everything changed. Not just how I looked in the mirror, but how I walked through the world. How I spoke to people. How I made decisions. How I dreamed about my future.

I wasn't just painting pictures anymore. I was painting my way to freedom. Freedom from shame, freedom from someone else's definition of beauty, freedom from the prison of self-hatred that had held me captive for so long.

And once I found that freedom, I knew I couldn't keep it to myself. I had to share it. I had to help other women find their way out of that same prison.

That's when I knew this journey was about more than just me. It was about every little Black girl who would ever look in the mirror and think she wasn't pretty enough. It was about every Black woman who had ever spent her grocery money on hair products because she thought she needed to be someone else to be worthy of love.

It was about changing the story not just for me, but for all of us.

Reflection Questions:

1. Can you recall a moment when you realized that a belief you held about yourself was actually something you had been taught by society rather than discovered on your own?
2. What would it feel like to see yourself represented positively in spaces where you've always felt invisible or underrepresented?

GUYLAINE'S ARTWORK

Photographer: Gregory Duhamel (https://just-afro.com)

From left to right, top to bottom: Afro Wheels; Cotton fro; barbewire; Angela; la Christiane; versatile 1.

AFRICAN HAIRSTYLES OF
YESTERDAY AND TODAY

Photographer: Norman Fredrick and others, https://africainthephotobook.com.

Chapter 6: Remembering the Crown

For so long, I thought I knew the story of Black hair history. But as I began to study it, I realized the version I carried was missing pieces—silenced voices, forgotten truths. The deeper I looked, the more the past came alive in ways I never expected. And once I saw it, I couldn't unsee it.

I had been natural for a while by the time I became an advocate, but I'll be honest—I was still carrying so much internalized shame and confusion about my hair journey. I knew the chemicals were bad for my health, I knew I looked beautiful and natural, but there was this nagging voice in the back of my head asking, "But why was it so hard? Why did it take me so long to get here? What was I really fighting against all those years?"

The answers came when I stumbled upon information about African hair traditions that nobody had ever taught me. What I discovered didn't just surprise me, it fundamentally changed how I saw myself and my ancestors.

What hit me hardest was learning what my hair actually meant. In African traditions, natural hair—coiled, textured, and reaching toward the sun—wasn't seen as difficult or unmanageable. It was spiritual. A conduit for divine connection. Powerful. Every style told a story: your tribe, your status, your life stage. A young boy's shaved head marked his passage to manhood. A woman's braids announced whether she was single, married, or widowed. I sat touching my own hair, thinking about all the times I'd been told it was "bad" or "difficult," and realized I'd spent decades trying to silence something that was meant to sing. That realization broke my heart and filled it with pride simultaneously.

Can you imagine? Our hair was like a language, a complex system of identity and communication that had been developed over thousands of years. Each twist, each braid, each pattern told a story about who you were, where you came from, what your status was in the community. It was beautiful, sophisticated, and deeply meaningful.

When our ancestors were enslaved and brought to the Americas, the first thing enslavers did was shave their hair—not for hygiene, but to erase identity. In one violent act, they stripped away the ability to recognize each other, to know who was from your tribe. Already separated from their families, languages, and everything familiar, our ancestors lost the one visible thing that marked them as distinctly African, distinctly themselves. For 400 years after, the message never changed: your hair is wrong, ugly, unprofessional, unacceptable. They didn't just cut our hair. They cut our connection to ourselves.

This research led me to discover an initiative in the United States called the Crown Act (Creating a Respectful and Open World for Natural Hair Act), and I was honestly surprised by what I learned. In the 21st century, we are still fighting for the right to wear our hair as it grows naturally from our scalps. The Crown Act was working to prohibit discrimination based on natural hair textures and styles in workplaces and schools. African American women introduced this act to their government, which then made it law.

The statistics were staggering. The 2021 CROWN Research Study for Girls showed that 86% of Black children had experienced hair discrimination before the age of 12. That's 12 years old! We taught children that their natural hair was wrong before they even reached their teenage years. Women were being fired from jobs for wearing their hair natural. Students were being suspended from school for wearing hairstyles deemed unacceptable.

I read story after story of Black women who had lost jobs, been denied promotions, or been told their natural hair was "unprofessional." There was a woman in a hotel who got fired for having locs. Students who were told their braids were distracting. Professionals who were passed over for leadership roles because their afros were deemed "too militant."

But you know what made me angry? Learning that in some places, the laws against natural hair were already on the books. I discovered that even in former French colonies like Guadeloupe and Martinique, there were laws stating that "woolly hair" wasn't presentable and had to be covered. This wasn't just about personal preference or beauty standards. This was systematic oppression. This was using our physical features as weapons against us, creating laws and social norms that made our natural selves literally illegal or socially unacceptable.

And the most insidious part? We internalized it. We believed it. When I finally went natural on television, it wasn't white people who criticized me the most—it was Black people saying, "Oh my God, what did you do to your hair?" We had been so thoroughly conditioned to reject our own natural beauty that we policed each other.

The psychological damage runs so deep. I was reading about colorism and texture bias within our own communities—how we've been taught to value lighter skin and straighter hair textures. I saw a video of a Black man telling a dark-skinned Black woman that she had "the audacity of a light-skinned girl" just for being confident. A Black man said that to a Black woman. That's how twisted our thinking had become.

But understanding this history didn't just make me angry—it made me proud. It helped me understand that when I chose to wear my natural hair, I wasn't just making a personal decision. I was reclaiming something that had been stolen from my ancestors. I was taking back a language that had been silenced for centuries.

The research also helped me understand the global nature of what we were experiencing. The natural hair movement wasn't just happening in America—it was happening all over the African diaspora. We were all waking up at the same time, all questioning the same lies we'd been told, all reclaiming the same stolen heritage.

I learned about the resistance movements throughout history—how, during the Black Power era of the late 1960s and 1970s, the afro became a symbol of pride and defiance. "Black is Beautiful" wasn't just a slogan—it was a revolutionary statement that directly challenged centuries of being told we were ugly.

In the Caribbean, including Guadeloupe, we were influenced by those American movements, but our context was different. Slavery had been abolished in Guadeloupe seventeen years earlier (1848) than in the United States (1865), but we were still colonized mentally and culturally. We were still trying to be French, still trying to fit European beauty standards, still believing that their way was the right way.

I remember the men in my family wearing afros during that era, inspired by what they saw happening in America. But for women, it took longer. We were still hot-combing our hair, still trying to make it straight and manageable. The resistance for Black women came later, and it continues to happen now.

Learning about this history has helped me understand my own journey in a different light. It wasn't that I was weak or vain for wanting straight hair all those years. I was responding to centuries of conditioning, to systems that were designed to make me reject myself. The fact that I eventually broke free wasn't just personal growth—it was an act of resistance.

I started wearing my hair in micro locs not just because they looked good, but because I was connecting to ancestral wisdom about how to care for textured hair. Each twist became a meditation, a way of honoring the women who came before me who knew how to work with hair like mine.

The funny thing is, once I stopped fighting my hair and started working with it, everything became easier. I stopped putting products on it, stopped trying to manipulate it into shapes it didn't want to hold. I just let it be what it was—alive, textured, reaching toward the sun like it was designed to do.

I became what you might call a "bad example" of hair maintenance because I do the opposite of everything I used to do. No chemicals, minimal products, and minimal manipulation. My hair had been mistreated for so many years that I decided the best thing I could do was leave it alone. And you know what? It thrived.

My approach became simple: treat my hair like I treat my body. Give it water for hydration, oil for nourishment, and gentle care. Don't torture it, don't force it, don't try to make it something it's not. Just let it live.

This research and journey have fundamentally changed how I see myself. My hair isn't just hair, it's a crown that connects me to my ancestors, a symbol of resistance against systems that tried to break us, and a celebration of the beauty that was always there but had been hidden under layers of shame and chemical processing.

When I look in the mirror now, I see more than just Guylaine. I see the legacy of African queens and warriors, of women who survived the Middle Passage with their dignity intact, of Civil Rights activists who used their hair as a weapon against oppression. I see the women who came before me who didn't have the freedom to wear their hair naturally, and I honor them by exercising the freedom they fought for.

But I also see the future. I see my daughter and the children in my community who will grow up seeing natural hair as normal and beautiful because we normalized it. I see young women who won't have to go through decades of chemical damage and self-hatred before they learn to love themselves.

Through my art, I try to tell this story. I have a painting called "Cotton" that addresses the horrible comparison between our hair and cotton—the same cotton our ancestors were forced to pick under the burning sun. In Guadeloupe, slaves worked in sugar cane fields, not cotton fields, so when I moved to America and learned about this comparison, it broke my heart and inspired my art.

Each painting I create is a small part of reclaiming our narrative, of telling our story from our perspective instead of letting others define us. When I paint a Black woman with beautiful natural hair, I'm not just creating art—I'm creating a counter-narrative to centuries of negative images.

I hope that my art might hang in someone's home or a museum 100 or 200 years from now. Someone might look at my paintings and say, "This was created during the natural hair movement of the early 21st century. This was when Black women were learning to love themselves again." That's the legacy I want to leave.

But the most important part of this journey has been sharing what I've learned. I wish someone had come to my school when I was little and told me that I was beautiful with my natural hair. I wish someone had explained the history, the significance, and the beauty of what grows naturally from my scalp.

That's why I speak about it now, why I share my story, why I encourage other women to do their own research and make their own choices. I'm not trying to force anyone to go natural—it took me 35 years to get there, and I understand that it's a deeply personal journey that everyone has to take in their own time.

But I want people to have the information. I want them to understand the risks of chemical processing, the beauty of natural hair, and the historical context of why we've been taught to hate ourselves. I want them to know that when they choose to embrace their natural hair, they're not just making a beauty choice—they're participating in an act of cultural reclamation and resistance.

The work isn't done. We still have so far to go. Even now, with more acceptance of natural hair, we're still bombarded with images that reinforce European beauty standards. Social media influencers still predominantly showcase straight hair and European features. The beauty industry still markets products based on changing rather than celebrating our natural textures.

But every woman who chooses to wear her hair naturally, every child who grows up seeing natural hair as beautiful, every workplace that changes its policies to be more inclusive—they're all part of dismantling a system that took centuries to build.

My hair journey taught me that healing isn't just personal—it's political, cultural, and spiritual. When I learned to love my hair, I also learned to love my Blackness, my heritage, and my place in a long line of strong women who had survived and thrived despite everything that was thrown their way.

My micro locs aren't just hair. They're a crown I've reclaimed, one that's carried generations of strength, pride, and story, waiting for me to see it for what it truly is. I see the wisdom of ancestors who knew how to care for hair like mine. I see the courage of women who fought for my right to wear it naturally. And I see the hope for future generations who will never have to question whether they're beautiful exactly as they are.

That's what remembering the crown really means—understanding that our natural hair was never the problem. The problem was a system that taught us to see our crowns as chains, our beauty as ugliness, our strength as weakness. But once you remember, once you truly understand what you're carrying on your head, everything changes.

You start walking differently. You start speaking differently. You start demanding the respect that was always your birthright. Because you're not just wearing hair—you're wearing history, heritage, and hope all twisted together in the most beautiful crown that nature could design.

Reflection Questions

1. **Internalized Messages**: What negative messages about your natural self did you internalize before you were old enough to question them? How do these early messages still influence your choices today?
2. **Your Crown**: What natural aspects of yourself have you been taught to see as flaws that might actually be sources of strength and beauty? How would your life change if you truly saw these as part of your crown?

Chapter 7: From Canvas to Congress

Sometimes the universe puts you exactly where you need to be, even when you think you're just dropping your daughter off at basketball practice.

Do you want to know how my art career really began? With a bold leap. A beautiful, necessary leap that changed the trajectory of my entire life.

It was 2019, and I was still finding my footing in America. My daughter was in basketball practice in Pembroke Pines, Florida, and I had time to kill. You know how it is when you're waiting for your kids—you can either sit in your car scrolling through your phone, or you can explore the world around you.

I chose to explore.

There was a gallery, Studio 18, in Pembroke Pines. One day, I walked in because I was curious, because I loved art, because something about the space called to me. Inside, there was this elderly man, very sweet and kind. The type of person who makes you feel welcome the moment you walk through the door.

He looked at me and asked, "Are you an artist?"

And I said, "No, no, no, I'm a journalist, but I love art."

We started talking, and there was something about his energy and genuine interest that made me open up. I told him about my growing passion for painting Black women, for telling the story of our hair that had been buried inside me for so long. I said, "You know what? I've been so ashamed of who I was for most of my life, and I realized that something has to come out. I need to express this. I need to paint these stories that nobody is telling."

I told him about my vision for a show I had been dreaming about—"From Embarrassment to Pride." That was going to be the title of my first solo exhibition, whenever that might happen. Someday. Maybe. If I ever got good enough. If I ever got brave enough.

That's when this woman appeared, seemingly out of nowhere—the gallery manager. She had been listening to our conversation from the back office, and she walked up to us with this excitement in her eyes.

"Oh my God," she said, "I was listening to your story. I love it! We have a Black History Month group show coming up. It's a group show in two weeks. I'd like to invite you to participate. Can I see what you've done?"

Two weeks! My heart started racing. I had three pieces. Three! I had just started painting seriously, and we're talking about three amateur paintings that I wasn't even sure were any good.

But you know what I did? I looked at that opportunity standing in front of me, and I felt the weight of all those years of playing small, all those times I had let fear make decisions for me. And I said, "Ten. I have ten pieces."

The bold leap to say that I had a collection of pieces came out so naturally, so confidently, that even I believed that I was an accomplished artist. The reality was that I blurted out that I had ten without thinking about it. Call it faith or ambition, once the words left my mouth, there was no taking them back.

Her eyes lit up. "Ten pieces? That's perfect! Can you bring them tomorrow?"

Now my heart was really racing. I said I couldn't bring them the next day because—and this part was true—I didn't have photos of all of them on my phone. I showed her the three pieces I did have photographed, and thank God, she loved them.

"These are beautiful," she said, studying the images on my phone. "The way you capture the hair, the expressions... Can you bring the rest on Monday or Tuesday?"

I needed that weekend to create the other seven. I needed every single hour of that weekend.

When I left that gallery, I didn't panic and go home. I didn't call anyone to confess what I had done. I went straight to the art supply store like a woman on a mission. I bought ten canvases—good quality ones, not the cheap ones I had been practicing on. I bought acrylic paint because I couldn't use oil—the drying process would take too long, and I literally had 48 hours to pull off what might have been the most ambitious art project of my life.

I painted for twelve hours a day, all weekend long. Twelve hours! I was like a woman possessed. I barely ate. I barely slept. I painted until my back ached, until my eyes burned, until my hands cramped. I painted like my life depended on it.

Because in a way, it did.

I had given myself this opportunity, this chance to step into the art world, and I wasn't going to waste it because I was scared or unprepared. I was going to make myself ready.

On Saturday morning, I began creating a painting of a woman with a beautiful afro. Sunday, I painted locs, braids, and twist-outs. I painted young faces and older ones. I painted joy, contemplation, and strength. I painted the hair stories I had been carrying in my heart, the faces I saw in my dreams, the beauty I was finally learning to recognize.

Were they masterpieces? Absolutely not. Were they good? Not really. But were they authentic? Were they full of passion and purpose and something that needed to be said? Yes. Absolutely yes.

On Monday morning, I loaded all ten pieces into my car and drove back to that gallery. My heart was pounding as I carried them inside, wondering if she would take one look and realize I was a fraud, wondering if this was the end of my art career before it had even begun.

She looked at each painting carefully, thoughtfully. I held my breath.

"I'll take four of them for the show," she said.

Four! Out of seven new pieces I had painted in a weekend, she wanted four for a Black History Month exhibition. I wanted to cry. I wanted to dance. I wanted to call someone and tell them what had just happened, but I was still keeping this dream close to my chest, still afraid to say out loud that I was trying to be an artist.

But I wasn't going to just show up to that exhibition like a wallflower. No ma'am! Although I was new to painting, I wasn't new to communication. I wasn't new to telling stories. And I had a story to tell. I called my friend who's a filmmaker and said, "Listen, I have my first art exhibition next week. You need to come and document this for me. I need an interview, some footage. How much do you charge?" I asked him. I paid him his fee, and he filmed everything.

In that video, which I still have, it appears to be my personal exhibition. You would never know it was a group show with other artists. You would never know that I was the newest and most inexperienced person in that room. You would never know that my paintings were created in a single weekend!

I had invited all my friends and called everyone I knew in Florida. I treated it like it was my debut at the Metropolitan Museum of Art in New York City. I was nervous when it was time to give my speech. Speaking in English about such a personal topic was terrifying for me, because I was still learning a lot about the language. Remember, I learned English in London over thirty years ago, and I had lost so much of it in the years between. The American accent was still challenging for me to understand, and expressing myself in a language that wasn't my native tongue about something so close to my heart—that was scary.

I was afraid people would ask me questions I couldn't answer, afraid I would stumble over words, afraid my French accent would be too thick, afraid they wouldn't understand what I was trying to say.

But I decided to be vulnerable, to be candid, to be completely honest about my journey. I just presented myself as I was and said, "This is my journey. This is where I've been, and this is where I'm going."

I told them about my childhood in France, about the first time my mother straightened my hair with a hot comb for my first Communion. I told them about the years of relaxers and weaves, about the shame I carried, about the health problems that forced me to go natural. I told them about moving to America and realizing that the struggle with hair was a universal experience among Black women.

I told them about discovering painting as a way to heal, as a way to see beauty in ourselves that we had been taught to hate. I told them that every painting was a prayer, every brushstroke an act of love for Black women who had been told they weren't beautiful enough.

And people connected with that story. They saw themselves in it. They could relate to the hot comb burns, to the chemical damage, to the years of believing they weren't pretty enough. There were women in the audience nodding and saying, "Amen." At the end of the evening, people were coming up to me, hugging me, telling me their own hair stories. Women were saying, "Oh my God, yes! I remember the hot comb!" They saw themselves in my journey, and suddenly, I realized this wasn't just about me anymore.

That experience gave me a confidence I had never had before. I walked out of that gallery thinking, I can do this. I can continue to do this. This matters. This story matters. These faces matter. I didn't sell any art that night, but I gained something more valuable than money. I gained the certainty that I was on the right path.

During the COVID-19 pandemic, when the world shut down and we all had to stay home, I had more time to focus on my art and research. Remember, I'm a journalist at heart, so I needed data. I needed to understand the full scope of what I was dealing with.

I had discovered different ethnicities and their hair traditions, ancient Egypt and its elaborate wigs and hair styling. I wanted to understand how locs became popular in Jamaica in the 1930s, particularly within the Rastafarian movement, as an anticolonial, Afrocentric spiritual practice. As the sociologist Anthony Synnot said in *Shame and Glory*, hair is a powerful symbol of individual and group identity: it's physical, it's personal, but also public rather than private.

I was diving deep into the hair story, learning everything I could, connecting dots I had never seen before. The more I learned, the more I understood that hair for Black people has never been just about hair. It's always been political. It's always been about power, resistance, and identity.

The state of California passed the first Crown Act in 2019, and other states started following. I tried to get in touch with the Crown Act organization because I wanted to support their work, learn from them, and be part of the movement. But they didn't reach back out to me fast enough, which I am not surprised by, because news of this was taking off, and I am sure they had many people trying to contact them. They did call me much later, after I had already started my own movement in France.

I spent those COVID years not just improving my painting technique, but also working on the business side of being an artist. I was battling serious imposter syndrome. I mean, who was I to call myself an artist? I had never gone to art school. I had never had formal training. I was just a journalist with paintbrushes and a story to tell.

I didn't even hang my own art in my house for the first two years. Can you imagine? I was painting these pieces that people were responding to, but I didn't feel worthy of displaying them in my own home.

I had to work on being professional, on presenting myself as a serious artist rather than someone who just painted as a hobby. I sold my first two pieces two months after my first exhibition, at the Joliet Historical Museum outside of Chicago, Illinois. I was happy, excited, and grateful. I met curators, spoke with people in the art world, and asked for advice on everything from the quality of paints to use to how to write an artist's statement.

I had to decide what kind of artist I wanted to be. An art curator in Florida told me that I had to make a choice. Either I was an artist who sold my work at craft fairs for $100 to $200, or I was an artist who showed in galleries and museums, which is a different positioning, a different strategy, and a different way of presenting myself and my work.

I chose the gallery route because I believed my message deserved to be presented to an audience that was different from the exclusively "crafts" type art lovers. I believed these faces and these stories deserved to be in broader spaces.

The advocacy part of my journey came in 2022, and it started with anger. Pure, righteous anger.

I was in Florida, reading a French newspaper online, just trying to stay connected to what was happening back home. I came across an article about a man named Aboubacar Traoré who was fired from his job in France due to his hairstyle. He was a flight attendant, with Air France since 1998, who grew his locs because he wanted to be himself.

For five years, he was forced to wear a wig to appear "professionally presentable," a daily mask against his identity. The day he said "enough" and showed up with his natural hair, he was grounded and banned from flying. This marked the beginning of a long, arduous, and painful legal battle to have his right to be himself recognized: labor court, rejection; appeal court, rejection; then, after ten years of persistence, the ruling of the Court of Cassation on November 23, 2022 came. Victory, but incomplete: the court upheld gender discrimination, ruling that what is tolerated for women is refused for men, without ever mentioning hair discrimination based on texture and origin. It was this "almost" that pierced me.

From this flaw arose my determination to initiate a bill explicitly targeting such discrimination. Aboubacar's story turned hair into a political issue for me; it transformed anger into work, so that no one would ever again have to disguise themselves in order to have the right to work.

I stared at that article and said to myself, "What? Why is this man being fired because of his hair? This is not normal! This is 2022—how can this still be happening?"

France had no Crown Act. There was no legal protection for people like Aboubacar. No recourse. No way to fight back against hair discrimination. That's when I realized I couldn't just paint pretty pictures and hope things would change. I had to do something bigger. I had to get involved in policy, in legislation, in the legal structures that either protect people or leave them vulnerable.

So I reached out to a congressman from Guadeloupe, Olivier Serva. I had come across him in person at my television news station, but I hadn't spoken with him. However, we were from the same place, and I thought maybe he would understand why this mattered.

I told him, "Hey, we should do something. We should create a bill to fight hair discrimination because this is not normal. Black people in France are being fired, denied jobs, and told their natural hair is unprofessional. We need legal protection."

He initially laughed at me. But I didn't see anything funny.

"What the hell are you talking about, Guylaine? You want me to go to French Congress?"

But I didn't give up. I couldn't give up. That man who got fired—he could have been my brother, my son, my friend. That discrimination could happen to any of us, and if we had no legal protection, we would all be vulnerable.

So I did what journalists do. I gathered evidence. I pulled data from the United States, from the United Kingdom, from anywhere I could find research on hair discrimination.

I found studies showing that one in two Black women feels pressured to straighten her hair for work. The Crown Act Workplace Research Study provided me with a wealth of information. It was a study that surveyed 2,990 women in the US, ages 25–64, and was almost evenly split among Black, Hispanic, and white women.

Most Black children experience discrimination about their hair before they're even teenagers. 81 percent of Black children in majority-white schools say they sometimes wish their hair were straight, and 100 percent of Black elementary school girls in majority-white schools experienced hair discrimination by age 10!

I contacted Michelle De Leon, who created World Afro Day in the UK and has been fighting hair discrimination there for years. She's truly the leader of the anti-hair discrimination movement in the UK, and she provided me with even more data and proof that this is a real problem affecting real people.

In France, this research was particularly challenging because our constitution says there are no races—we're all just French. So we don't have official statistics about discrimination against Black people because officially, Black people don't exist as a separate category. But we all know discrimination happens. We all live it.

I compiled all this information—studies from the US, research from the UK, and stories from France—and created a comprehensive file documenting the reality of hair discrimination.

I wrote it up professionally and sent it to the congressman's assistant, Lovely.

But I still needed expert support. I needed legal minds who understood discrimination law, who could help us navigate the complex process of creating legislation in a country where race officially doesn't exist.

That's when I was introduced to Professor Wendy Greene from Drexel University in Philadelphia. She's one of the architects of the Crown Act, a specialist in civil rights law, someone who has dedicated her career to fighting discrimination in all its forms.

When I called Professor Greene and explained what I wanted to do—create the first national hair discrimination law in the world—she didn't hesitate. She said yes immediately. She understood the importance of what we were trying to accomplish.

She helped us understand hair discrimination from a legal perspective. She helped us figure out how to write a law in France, where the constitution doesn't recognize racial categories. She showed us how to frame the issue in terms of individual dignity and human rights rather than racial protection.

Professor Greene was so committed to this cause that she agreed to come with me to France in November 2023. Can you imagine? An American law professor traveling to France to help create legislation that protects Black people's right to wear their natural hair. Natasha Gaspard, a New York Emmy Award-winning television producer, founder of ManeMoves, and advocate of the natural hair movement, also came with us.

The congressman organized a big conference around this proposed bill. We had doctors explaining the health damage from chemical hair products. We had dermatologists talking about scalp damage and alopecia. We had authors and researchers presenting the historical context of hair discrimination.

We had businesswomen who had created natural hair product lines explaining why they felt compelled to offer alternatives to harmful chemicals. We had educators talking about the psychological impact on children when they're told their natural hair is unprofessional or inappropriate.

Twenty specialists and over 400 people attended the French Congress meeting. The event was sold out! People were hungry for this conversation, ready to finally address something that had been hiding in plain sight for generations.

The energy in that room was electric. You could feel the shift happening, the recognition that this wasn't just about vanity or personal preference—this was about human dignity, about the right to exist authentically in the world without fear of punishment.

After months of preparation, research, legal consultations, and political maneuvering, the bill was officially presented to French Congress in March 2024. I bought my own plane ticket—this was my money, my investment in this cause—and flew to France to sit in that chamber and watch those elected officials debate legislation I had helped create. Legislation that began with my anger over one man's firing, my research as a journalist, and my determination to change things for future generations.

It was broadcast on television. People were watching from all over France and the French Antilles. I sat in the gallery looking down at those congressmen and women, many of whom had probably never thought about hair discrimination before this moment.

The debate was intense. I listened to the arguments both for and against. Some congressmen said, "We have so many problems in France. People are struggling with unemployment, with the economy, and with housing. What the hell are you bringing us here? We don't have to copy everything Americans do. This is not our problem. This is an American problem that you're trying to import to France."

Olivier Serva was like a lion fighting back; he argued that discrimination is discrimination, regardless of where it happens. That French citizens deserve protection from prejudice based on their appearance. That children shouldn't have to choose between their heritage and their education. The others were saying that there is already a law against discrimination in the French Constitution. They pushed back and claimed that there was no need to add a law on top of the other law, but Serva kept fighting.

I was sitting there trying not to react, because the guards had warned us—no movements, no facial expressions, no reactions of any kind, or they would remove us from the chamber. The protocol was strict, and they were watching us carefully.

But how do you control yourself when they're talking about your life, your identity, your people, your children's future? How do you sit still when some of them are dismissing your pain as unimportant, as foreign, as not worthy of their attention?

I was pretty animated during the debate, speaking up to myself in agreement or disagreement. The security guard came to me twice during the discussion and said, "We're going to remove you if you don't control yourself." I was trying so hard to keep my face neutral, but inside I was screaming, crying, praying, and hoping.

After two hours of debate, it was time to vote. The chamber got quiet. The clerk began the formal process. My heart was beating so fast I thought everyone could hear it. I saw on the screen in the prestigious building that it passed with a majority vote. Victory! When they announced that French Congress had voted to pass the law, I almost lost it completely. I wanted to jump up and scream, cry, and thank God all at the same time.

It was historic for so many reasons. The Crown Act was first passed in California in 2019 and has since been adopted in approximately 25 states in America. But those are state laws, regional protections, not a national mandate.

In France, we don't have states. When something passes French Congress, it becomes national law. France became the first country in the world to pass national legislation protecting people from hair discrimination.

The first country in the world!

We proved that change is possible. We proved that one person with a vision, determination, and the courage to speak up, conduct research, and build coalitions can create legislation that protects millions of people.

Of course, our work isn't finished yet. The bill still has to pass the Senate and be signed by France's president to become law. As of the time of the writing of this book, it hasn't happened yet. We're currently looking for senators who will champion it in the Senate.

But we made history that day. We addressed an issue that many people thought was trivial, dismissing it as vanity, and elevated it to the level of national policy. We said that human dignity matters, that children's self-esteem matters, that the right to exist authentically in the world without fear of discrimination matters.

I went from a woman who was ashamed of her hair to someone sitting in French Congress watching lawmakers debate legislation I helped create. From canvas to Congress—that's a journey I never imagined I would take.

But let me tell you what that experience taught me about the power of one voice, one story, one person willing to step outside their comfort zone and demand change.

When I first reached out to Congressman Serva, I was just a painter with a passion project. I had no political connections, no legal background, no experience in advocacy or legislation. What I had was righteous anger, solid research, and an unshakeable belief that things could be different.

The process of getting that bill to the floor wasn't easy. There were months of meetings, phone calls, and emails back and forth. There were times when I thought it would never happen, when the political machinery seemed too slow, too complicated, too resistant to change.

But every time I felt like giving up, I would remember Aboubacar Traoré, who wasn't permitted to wear his natural hairstyle at his job with Air France. I would think about all the Black children in French schools being told their hair was inappropriate, all the Black women being passed over for jobs because their natural hair didn't fit someone else's idea of professional appearance.

I would look at my own paintings—those faces I had learned to love, those crowns I had learned to celebrate—and I would remember that this fight wasn't just about policy. It was about every little Black child who would ever look in the mirror and wonder if she was beautiful enough. It was about changing the conversation from "fix yourself to fit in" to "the world needs to make space for who you are."

The day of the vote, sitting in that chamber, I kept thinking about my journey. I thought about that 9-year-old girl getting her ear burned by a hot comb for her first Communion. I thought about the teenager painting over her pain with relaxers and weaves. I thought about the young woman building a business around helping other women achieve the same transformation I thought we all needed.

And then I thought about the woman who picked up a paintbrush in Florida and decided to paint love letters to Black women who had never seen their beauty reflected to them.

All of those versions of me led to that moment. All of that pain, all of that learning, all of that growth—it was preparation for something bigger than I could have imagined.

When the vote passed, and France became the first country in the world to enact national hair discrimination legislation, I realized something profound: our personal healing can become a collective liberation.

My journey from self-hatred to self-love didn't end with me loving myself. It became a pathway for legal protection for millions of people. My art didn't just hang on gallery walls—it became visual evidence in support of legislation. My story didn't just help me heal—it helped change the law.

However, the real victory wasn't the vote count, the media coverage, or the historical significance. The real victory was knowing that because of this law, little Black girls in France won't have to choose between their heritage and their education. Black professionals won't have to chemically alter their hair to be considered for promotions. Parents won't have to worry that their children will be discriminated against at school because of how their hair grows naturally.

That's what systemic change looks like. It's not just about individual transformation—though that's important. It's about changing the structures, the laws, the policies that either protect people or leave them vulnerable.

The media response was interesting. Some outlets celebrated it as historic civil rights legislation. Others questioned whether it was necessary, whether hair discrimination was really a serious problem. But the fact that we were having the conversation at all meant we had already won something important.

We had taken an issue that had been hiding in beauty salons, bathrooms, and kitchen tables—whispered conversations about shame, pain, and the cost of conformity—and brought it into the light of public discourse.

We had said out loud what many people had been thinking privately: that requiring people to alter their natural appearance chemically to be considered professional is a form of discrimination. That telling children their hair is inappropriate is a form of psychological harm. Building entire industries around the premise that Black people need to be fixed is a form of economic exploitation.

And we had done something about it.

Since the bill passed Congress, I've been contacted by activists in other countries, such as South Africa and Ghana, who want to know how we achieved it, what strategies were effective, and what obstacles we encountered. Can you believe that African countries have their own hair discrimination issues? This shows you how deeply rooted colonization is in the psyche of Black people all over the world. There's a ripple effect happening—people in Canada, in the UK, in other parts of the Caribbean are looking at what France accomplished and asking, "Why not us too?"

That's the thing about breakthrough moments—they don't just change the place where they happen. They change what other people believe is possible. They expand the realm of what can be imagined, what can be fought for, and what can be won.

I've also been invited to speak at conferences, universities, and community organizations about the intersection of art and activism. People want to know how painting led to policy, how personal healing became a catalyst for political action, and how someone with no legal background managed to help create legislation.

The answer is simple, even if the process wasn't: you start where you are, with what you have, and you don't let anyone convince you that your story doesn't matter.

My paintings provided a platform for me to discuss hair discrimination. My research gave me credibility to speak to lawmakers. My lived experience gave me authenticity that couldn't be questioned. But most importantly, my willingness to be vulnerable and share my pain and healing publicly created connections with other people who had lived similar experiences.

And when people connect around shared pain and shared hope, when they realize they're not alone in their struggles, that's when movements begin.

Professor Greene, who became not just a collaborator but a friend through this process, taught me something important about social change. She showed me that progress doesn't happen because perfect people make perfect arguments to perfect audiences. Progress happens because imperfect people with compelling stories find ways to connect with other imperfect people who are ready to imagine something different.

That's exactly what happened with our hair discrimination law. We didn't have perfect research, though we had good research. We didn't have a perfect political strategy, though we learned as we went. We didn't have perfect media coverage, though we received enough attention to matter.

What we had was a compelling story about human dignity, solid evidence that discrimination was happening, and the persistence to keep pushing even when people told us it wasn't important enough, wasn't French enough, wasn't worth the political capital.

We dared to believe that Black children's self-esteem was worth fighting for at the highest levels of government. We had the conviction that economic fairness mattered, that women shouldn't have to spend disproportionate amounts of their income just to be considered for employment.

And we had the vision to see that this was bigger than hair—it was about the right to exist authentically in the world without fear of punishment.

As I write this, the bill is being considered by the Senate. I'm cautiously optimistic, but I'm also prepared for the reality that political processes are slow, that there will be more obstacles, and that we might need to fight this battle in multiple venues before achieving a final victory.

However, I'm no longer the same person who began this journey. I'm not the woman who was afraid to call herself an artist, who was ashamed of her natural hair, who thought her story didn't matter.

I'm someone who has learned that personal transformation and social change are not separate processes—they're interconnected parts of the same revolution. I'm someone who knows that art can be activism, that healing can be a political act, and that loving yourself can be a radical act that ripples out to change laws, policies, and the lives of people you'll never meet.

Sometimes people ask me if I ever imagined this journey would lead where it has led. The answer is no—I could never have imagined sitting in French Congress watching lawmakers debate legislation I helped create. I could never have imagined that the paintings I created in my Florida apartment would become part of a civil rights campaign.

But that's the thing about authentic living—you don't know where it will take you. You know that you can't keep living as someone else, wearing masks that don't fit, pretending to be satisfied with systems that diminish your humanity.

All I wanted to do was paint beautiful Black women with their natural hair. All I wanted was to heal my own relationship with the mirror, to find peace with the face and hair God gave me. I never knew that art would lead me to advocacy, that my personal journey would become a political movement, that my story would help change the law for millions of people around the world.

But that's the thing about authenticity—when you start living your truth, when you start creating from your authentic self, when you stop trying to fit into spaces that were never designed for you and start creating spaces that celebrate who you are—you never know how far that truth will travel or how many people it will set free.

From embarrassment to pride. From canvas to Congress. From self-hatred to self-love to liberation for others. That's the journey that begins when you decide you're worth fighting for. Not just personally, but politically. Not just individually, but collectively. Not just for yourself, but for everyone who shares your struggle and deserves your courage.

Reflection Questions:

1. What issues have you experienced personally that you think deserves broader attention or even policy change?
2. How comfortable are you with using your voice or platform to advocate for causes you believe in, even when others might dismiss them as unimportant?

FRENCH CONGRESS

November 16th, 2023 Hair Discrimination Conference held by French Congress in Paris.

Chapter 8: From Pain to Policy

The journey from pain to policy isn't easy, and anyone who tells you it is hasn't actually walked that path. You'll face people who don't believe your issue matters, who think you're being too sensitive or making mountains out of molehills. You'll face many obstacles and hurdles. You'll have moments where the system seems so rigged against you that giving up feels like the only reasonable option.

There will be days when you question whether you're the right person to lead this fight, whether someone else could do it better or faster or with less drama. There will be nights when you lie awake thinking about all the people depending on you, all the Mr. Traorés, congresswomen, and little girls who need this change to happen, and the weight of that responsibility will feel crushing.

But when you know your purpose, when you've found your calling, when you understand that your personal pain is connected to a larger pattern of injustice—you keep going. Not because it's easy or you're guaranteed success, not because people will always appreciate your efforts either, but because the alternative is unconscionable.

Because somewhere out there, another Mr. Traoré is wearing a wig to keep his job, spending his morning commute transforming himself into something more palatable for his employers. Another woman is straightening her hair before an interview because she's been taught that her natural texture is unprofessional. Another little girl is learning to hate what grows from her head, internalizing the message that her authentic self isn't acceptable.

And they deserve better. We all deserve better. We deserve to exist in professional spaces without apology, without compromise, without the exhausting performance of respectability that demands we shrink ourselves to make others comfortable. We deserve to exist as our authentic selves.

What I learned through this process is that systemic change requires both personal courage and strategic thinking. It's not enough to be angry about injustice, though anger is often the fuel that gets you started. You must channel that anger into research, into building coalitions, and into understanding how power works and how to navigate it effectively.

I also learned that you can't do this work alone, no matter how passionate you are. I needed Lovely to understand the personal impact of hair discrimination. I needed Dr. Greene to share her expertise on the CROWN Act. I needed the brave congresswoman Fanta Berete to tell her story publicly. I needed Mr. Traoré to put a face on the policy we were trying to change. Each person brought something essential that I couldn't provide by myself.

The work isn't finished. Even with the bill's passage in French Congress, we're still waiting for Senate approval as of the time of this book's publication. But the conversation has started. The precedent has been set. Other advocates in other countries are already reaching out, asking how they can replicate this model in their own legislative systems. This encourages me and gives me hope that what we're doing is making a difference.

That's how change really works. It does not work as a single dramatic moment, but as a series of small victories that build momentum over time. Every testimony shared, every study cited, and every person who decides to stop straightening their hair for job interviews is part of a larger transformation.

Looking back now, I can see how every experience in my journey led to this moment. The pain of being told my natural hair wasn't professional enough. The gradual awakening to the systemic nature of the problem. The research that turned personal grievance into a policy proposal. The political maneuvering that turned the proposal into law. Although the journey was tough, this passion against hair discrimination opened the door for me to do my advocacy work through my art.

Each step was necessary, even the difficult ones. Especially the difficult ones. Because real change doesn't come from staying in our comfort zones, it comes from people who are willing to be uncomfortable, to risk ridicule, to face down powerful institutions and demand better.

If there's one thing I want people to take from this story, it's that your pain has purpose if you're willing to transform it. The discrimination you've faced, the injustices you've endured, and the ways you've been made to feel less than can all become fuel for creating change that extends far beyond your individual experience.

You don't have to be a politician, a lawyer, or an expert to start this work. You just have to be willing to say, "This isn't right, and I'm going to do something about it." You have to be willing to research, to build relationships, to persist when people dismiss you, to find your allies and work with them even when they disappoint you.

The world needs your voice, your perspective, your willingness to fight for what's right. Some systems need changing, policies need challenging, conversations need having. And maybe—just maybe—your personal struggle is the key that unlocks progress for countless others facing the same challenges.

That's what empowerment really looks like. Not just accepting yourself, but creating a world where acceptance isn't necessary because discrimination isn't tolerated. Not just loving your natural hair, but making it illegal for others to punish you for it.

Each story and testimony I had read online regarding hair discrimination felt like a mirror of my own experience. There was a teacher in Alabama who was told her locs were a "distraction" to students. A banker in Texas was passed over for promotion until she started wearing her hair straight. A college student was sent home from her internship because her braids didn't fit the company's "corporate image."

As I scrolled through these testimonies, my heart was racing. All these years, I thought I was being too sensitive, that maybe I was imagining the microaggressions, the subtle ways people looked at my hair, the assumptions they made about my professionalism. But here was proof—documented, legal proof—that this discrimination was real, widespread, and finally being addressed.

Whether you're Black or mixed-race identifying as Black in France, the US, England, Brazil, wherever you are, you have likely been a victim of discrimination based on your hair. For me, hair discrimination is just as bad as skin discrimination. It's like being discriminated against for the color of your skin because, let's be honest, our hair texture is directly connected to our racial identity.

The global nature of this discrimination hit me like a truck. This wasn't just an American problem that I could observe from afar. This wasn't just a Caribbean problem affecting my home islands. This was everywhere. Black people everywhere were being told that what grows naturally from our heads is somehow wrong, unprofessional, unacceptable.

The thing is, when you know you're meant for this, when conviction fuels every step, quitting simply isn't an option. You find another way. You push harder. You make them listen.

I became a detective of discrimination, a scholar of systemic bias. I delved into the Dove study, which involved approximately 2,000 women in the US—did you know that two out of three Black women change their hairstyle before a job interview? Two out of three! They're not even being asked to do it by employers. They assume they're not presentable as they are. They believe they'll have a better chance of getting the job with straightened hair, which looks more like what white women have.

Think about what that means for a moment. Before these women even walk into the room, they're already compromising their authenticity because they know the system is biased against them. They're spending hours and sometimes hundreds of dollars to chemically alter or heat-style their hair because they've internalized the message that their natural state isn't acceptable in professional spaces.

The statistics were staggering. Black women were three times more likely than white women to be sent home from work because of their hair. They were 80% more likely to change their hair to fit in at work. And these weren't just entry-level positions—this was happening to executives, teachers, doctors, lawyers. No level of education or success could protect Black women from hair discrimination.

Then I came across this incredible UK study called The Hair Discrimination Study, part of the Hair Equality Report (2020) by World Afro Day and De Montfort University—and it flipped the script entirely.

In the study, instead of asking Black employees about their experiences with discrimination, the researchers interviewed employers, HR managers, and decision-makers. They showed them two identical resumes with photos—women and men with straight hair versus those with locs or braids: the same qualifications, the same experience, the same education. Guess what? 70 percent said they would choose the person with straight hair. 70 percent!

That wasn't us claiming to be victims—that was them admitting their bias. That was proof that the discrimination wasn't in our heads, wasn't us being "too sensitive" or "playing the race card." That was empirical evidence that our hair was costing us opportunities.

In France, we specifically can't do studies based on race to directly influence legislation because, officially, we don't have Black, white, or Latino people. The French ideal of "colorblindness" means we're all just French citizens, regardless of the obvious racial disparities that exist in our society. It sounds progressive on paper, but in practice, it means we can't document discrimination as effectively as other countries can.

So I had to be creative. I had to bring studies from overseas to prove that the same thing was happening in France. I compiled research from the US, the UK, Brazil, Canada, and anywhere that had documented the reality of hair discrimination. I created a comprehensive dossier that showed this wasn't just an isolated problem in one country, but a global pattern of bias against Black hair textures and styles.

I spent weeks building this case, working late into the night, printing articles, highlighting statistics, organizing testimonies. My dining room table became mission control for what would eventually become French legislation. I felt like a lawyer preparing for the most important case of my career, except this wasn't about money or professional advancement—this was about dignity, about the right to exist authentically in professional spaces.

Serva's assistant, Lovely, actually read through everything I had compiled. She didn't just dismiss it or file it away. She connected with the issue on a personal level. She understood, in a way that Serva couldn't, what this legislation could mean for Black women and our families. She pushed Serva, telling him this was a real issue for Black women especially. And you know what? Half his team thought we were crazy, that people in French Congress would make fun of us. Can you imagine? They were worried about being ridiculed for trying to protect people from discrimination. That tells you everything you need to know about how seriously hair discrimination is taken, even by people who should know better.

But the other half of his team said we had to do it, even if it seemed impossible. Even if it made them look foolish, even if they didn't fully understand the depth of the problem, and that's when I learned something important about change: you don't need everyone to believe in your cause from the beginning. You just need enough people to be willing to take a chance on doing the right thing.

We started planning this massive event at French Congress. This wasn't going to be a quiet committee meeting or a backroom negotiation. We were going to make noise. We were going to make sure people paid attention. I reached out to Wendy Greene, one of the architects of the CROWN Act in the US, because if we were going to undertake this effort, we needed expertise from someone who had already won this fight.

Dr. Greene is incredible, and I don't use that word lightly. Her parents sacrificed a lot for their activism during the Civil Rights movement, and fighting for justice is literally in her blood. When I called her and explained what we were trying to do in France, she didn't hesitate. "Of course I'll help," she said. "This fight doesn't stop at borders."

We had a Zoom meeting with Serva, who spoke a bit of English, although French is his primary language. Lovely translated, I took notes in French and English, and Professor Greene shared her experience with advocating for the CROWN Act. It was a beautiful moment of international solidarity, all of us from different continents and backgrounds united by the understanding that our hair is a political statement, whether we want it to be or not.

The event was incredible. We were sold out—completely packed with specialists talking about the economics of hair discrimination, the social impact, the psychological effects on children who learn early that their natural hair is somehow wrong. We had economists explaining how much money Black women spend annually trying to make their hair "acceptable" for professional settings. We had psychologists discussing the mental health impacts of constantly feeling like your natural self isn't good enough.

The room was electric. You could feel the energy of people who had never seen their experiences validated at this level. There were Black women in the audience who expressed relief that they were finally being heard. Finally, someone was saying out loud what they had been feeling their whole lives.

The media attention helped us enormously, because suddenly people were talking about hair discrimination everywhere—on social media, in newspapers, on television. Serva, as a seasoned politician, knew how to navigate the media landscape effectively. He went on television, radio shows, and gave interviews to newspapers, bringing visibility to the issue in ways I never could have alone. The coverage was extensive—more than we'd dared to hope for.

Here's where I learned an important but difficult lesson about advocacy work and political partnerships. In the whirlwind of media appearances, the narrative sometimes shifted in ways that felt uncomfortable. Friends and colleagues who were aware of my years of work on this issue would call, asking if this was the project I'd initiated. The recognition I'd hoped for didn't always come in the way I'd imagined.

I had to navigate those feelings—the disappointment when my name wasn't mentioned, the frustration of watching coverage that didn't acknowledge the grassroots origins of the work. It was a reminder that in politics, the messenger sometimes overshadows the message, even when the message is what truly matters.

But what I came to understand is that changing systems requires working within them, even when they're imperfect. Serva had access to platforms and political capital that I didn't. His visibility brought attention to hair discrimination that might have taken years to achieve otherwise. Sometimes, progress requires compromise, which means letting go of personal recognition for the sake of the larger goal.

Despite how I felt, Serva fought for the law when it mattered. Politics is a game of give and take, and he knew how to play it. He made deals, called in favors, and worked his relationships to get the votes we needed. And that's the complicated reality of creating change through institutional channels—sometimes you have to work with people you don't initially trust because they have access to power that you don't. When it came time for the vote, a lot of those from the right-wing party didn't show up because hair discrimination wasn't their priority. Out of the usual 200 people, maybe 80 were there. But those who were there heard powerful testimony.

There was Congresswoman Fanta Berete, who took the stand and shared her story. Her mother was from Africa, and even though they were from a modest background and her mother was working very hard to make ends meet, she would buy fake braided hair so that her daughter could look "presentable" and fit into society. A congressional colleague even boldly touched her hair without her permission to compliment her on how pretty it was to him. In 2024! A sitting congresswoman receiving messages like that.

When I met Mr. Traoré, the man whose story had started this entire journey for me, at the French Congress meeting, he thanked me. He had flown in from Spain, where he now lives after leaving France following his ordeal. Seeing him in person and hearing his voice was like closing a circle that had started two years earlier when I read about his case.

He told me his full story with details that hadn't been in the newspaper article. When Air France hired him nine years ago, he had very short hair, almost a buzz cut. They told him even that was too much, not "neat" enough for their standards. When he grew his hair out into neat, well-maintained locs, they said those weren't acceptable either. His hair was too Black, too ethnic, too much of a reminder that not everyone who worked for their "prestigious" airline looked like the white French ideal.

So you know what he did? He bought a wig. For five years, he wore an ugly, uncomfortable wig to work every single day. He showed me pictures, and honestly, the wig was terrible. It looked nothing like real hair, nothing like him. But he wore it because he needed his job. After all, he had bills to pay, and he thought this humiliation was the price of professional success.

He called it his dignity that they had taken from him. "They didn't just discriminate against my hair," he told me. "They made me participate in my own dehumanization. Every morning when I put on that wig, I was denying who I was to make them comfortable."

When he finally decided he couldn't do it anymore, when he couldn't look at himself in the mirror one more time wearing that synthetic hair, he took off the wig and went to work as himself. Unfortunately, he was no longer able to fly due to the airline's decision.

That moment—seeing him, hearing his story, knowing that my reading that article about him had started this whole journey— that's when I knew with absolute certainty that I was exactly where I was supposed to be. This wasn't just about me anymore. This wasn't even just about France. This was about all of us, everywhere, who had been told that our natural selves weren't good enough.

Due to the current political turmoil in France, everything's on hold for the moment. The legislative process has been disrupted, our momentum interrupted, our timeline thrown into chaos. It's frustrating, but it's also a reminder that progress isn't linear. Change doesn't happen on our schedule, according to our plans.

What I want you to understand is that becoming an advocate didn't make me fearless. It didn't eliminate my insecurities or heal all my wounds or make me immune to discrimination. What it did was give me a framework for understanding my experiences, a community of support, and a sense of purpose that transcended my individual struggles.

It transformed my relationship with my own story. Instead of something I wanted to hide or forget, my journey with hair became something I was proud to share. Every struggle, every setback, every moment of pain or confusion—all of it became meaningful because it contributed to a larger narrative of resistance and transformation.

The woman who learned about the CROWN Act and Mr. Traoré's story in 2022 was not the same woman who had started wearing natural hair years earlier. That earlier version of me was focused on personal acceptance, on learning to love myself despite what the world said. This new version of me was focused on changing what the world says, on creating spaces where self-love isn't an act of rebellion but simply the baseline of how we treat ourselves and others.

This is what empowerment really looks like. Not just feeling good about yourself, but using your experience to create change. Not just healing your own wounds, but working to prevent future wounds. Not just surviving discrimination, but fighting to dismantle it.

When people ask me how I found my purpose, I tell them I didn't find it—it found me. It was always there in my pain, in my struggles, in my experiences with discrimination. I just had to recognize it, claim it, and channel it into action.

Right now, in offices, schools, and homes around the world, someone is making the painful calculation that their authentic self isn't acceptable. Someone is spending money they don't have on products and services to transform what grows naturally from their head. Someone is teaching their daughter that certain textures need to be "fixed" before they are considered beautiful. Someone is accepting less than they deserve because they've been convinced that who they are isn't enough.

Your pain has purpose, too. Your struggles have meaning. Your story has power. The question is: what will you do with it?

Reflection Questions

1. **Identifying Your Moment of Clarity**: Guylaine's "moment" came when she read about Mr. Traoré's experience. Think about a time when you realized a personal struggle you faced was actually part of a larger

systemic issue. How did this realization change your perspective on your own experience?

2. **From Victim to Advocate**: Guylaine transformed from someone experiencing discrimination to someone fighting against it systemically. What personal challenges or injustices have you experienced that could benefit others if you chose to advocate for change? What's holding you back from taking that step?

Chapter 9: The Community of Empowerment

Change always feels personal at first. You think it's your struggle, your burden to bear. But the moment you stand up and speak out, you find yourself surrounded by voices, stories, and a community that's been waiting for you all along.

After our first meeting at French Congress in 2023, when they debated the bill, something beautiful happened that I hadn't expected. We created more than just a legislative moment—we created a movement. A real, breathing community of women from all over Europe, Africa, the Caribbean, and everywhere our stories had traveled through media coverage. We had testimony pouring in online from people who had been waiting their whole lives for someone to say what we were saying.

That day at Congress, after all the formal presentations and political speeches were done, we went to a restaurant together. Can you imagine? Here were all these women who had never met before, but we were connected by something deeper than friendship; we were connected by shared experience, by the understanding that comes from living the same discrimination.

Some hairdressers had their own stories. Some stylists understood the economics of hair discrimination better than any economist could. There were women from diverse professions, backgrounds, and walks of life. But every single one of us had a story about our hair. Every single Black woman there had experienced something that made them feel less than, unprofessional, unwelcome in spaces where they had every right to belong.

As we sat around those restaurant tables sharing our experiences, I realized something profound: I wasn't alone in this experience, and more importantly, none of us had to be alone anymore. We were building something together, creating a community that could support and strengthen each other.

The media attention had helped us enormously because suddenly people were talking about hair discrimination everywhere—on social media, in newspapers, on television. The Afro-Caribbean community in France was paying attention, sharing their own stories, adding their voices to our chorus. What had started as my individual journey to understand and challenge discrimination had become a collective awakening.

One story that really stuck with me came from a young woman who had tried to get her hair done at a regular French salon, not a specifically Black or Caribbean salon, but just a regular neighborhood hairdresser. When she walked in and asked for service, they told her, "We're sorry, but we don't do that kind of hair."

Think about what that means in the context of French society. France prides itself on being a nation where race doesn't officially exist, where everyone born there is simply French, period. No racial categories, no ethnic distinctions—just French citizens. But here was this woman, a French citizen, French-educated, French in every legal and cultural sense, being told that her hair was somehow different, somehow not French enough for a French salon.

The problem wasn't just workplace discrimination; it was systemic exclusion at every level. French hairdressing schools don't teach students how to work with textured hair, with kinky hair, with hair that doesn't fit the European standard. So when Black women try to access basic services, they're pushed toward their own communities. They are restricted to only African salons or stylists who specialize in "our kind" of hair.

But if there's no race in France, if we're all just French, then why should Black women be limited to Black salons? Why should our hair be treated as something separate or special that requires different training and different spaces? The contradiction was glaring once you started looking at it clearly.

As our community grew and our conversations deepened, we realized that hair discrimination affected more than just Black women. We began hearing from people we hadn't expected, and their testimony opened our eyes to the broader scope of this problem.

There was a blonde woman who told us she couldn't get promoted because her manager said that being blonde doesn't look serious enough for leadership. Can you believe that? A woman's competence and qualifications were dismissed because of the color of her hair. We heard from people who faced constant jokes and microaggressions because they were bald, comments that might seem harmless but that created hostile work environments. Some employers wouldn't hire bald people for customer-facing positions, claiming their appearance wasn't professional enough.

We received testimony about age discrimination through hair. People with gray hair being told they are too old for certain positions, being pressured to dye their hair to appear younger and more "dynamic." Hair discrimination often hides behind ageism, but it is still a form of discrimination nonetheless.

Women from North African and Middle Eastern backgrounds also shared their experiences. My friend from Morocco told me she would never go to work without getting a blowout first, because when she wore her natural curly, fluffy hair, colleagues would ask her, "What's wrong with you? Did you stick your finger in an electrical socket?" The mockery, assumptions, and pressure to conform to a straight-haired standard—it was all so familiar.

People with red hair told us about the songs and rhymes French children learn that mock redheads, the stereotypes and prejudices that follow them through life. Even something as seemingly innocent as hair color became a source of discrimination and exclusion.

This broader understanding became our secret weapon in the legislative process. Because France doesn't recognize racial categories, we couldn't go to Congress and say, "We Black people experience hair discrimination." We had to frame it differently. We had to show that hair discrimination affects many French citizens across different backgrounds and characteristics.

That's how we were able to build such a strong case. We weren't asking for special protection for one group—we were asking for basic dignity for all French people who had been discriminated against because of their hair texture, color, or style. It was brilliant, really, the way Professor Greene helped us navigate this legal landscape.

Building this community wasn't easy, especially since I was living in the United States while trying to maintain connections across an ocean. Community building requires consistency, regular phone calls, constant social media engagement, and being present for people when they need support. It's hard to do that when you're working full-time and dealing with time zone differences as well as having to travel back and forth regularly.

But every time I went to Paris, I made sure to meet with our community. I connected with the influencers, business owners, activists, and everyday women who were part of our movement.

We would update each other on our progress, share new developments, and support each other's individual projects.

I stayed in touch with Lovely (from Serva's office) and with the other women from our original French Congress meeting. We kept our group chat active, sharing information and opportunities. What amazed me was how this community started reaching beyond France's borders. I connected with Michelle De Leon, who created a global celebration of afro hair called World Afro Day, which occurs every September 15th. It's a day of celebration and education about culture and identity for those with African roots. Suddenly, I was part of a global network of people working on similar issues.

Dr. Charlene Makita from South Africa reached out, seeking assistance in developing legislation to address hair discrimination in her country. Another author, Gloria Tabi from Ghana, the author of several books that address hair discrimination, contacted me with the same request. Each time, I was honest about my limitations—I'm an artist, not a lawyer—but I could share our process and connect them with Professor Greene, who was always willing to lend her legal expertise.

There are other remarkable women, perhaps not as widely known, who are transforming the conversation around Black hair in powerful ways. Célia's natural hair line, Chebhair, is now stocked in pharmacies across France. A woman named Ghana partners with major French salons and is helping train stylists in the science and artistry of textured hair. Eva's Hair fosters community through its annual Textured Hair Day in Paris—a vibrant gathering where culture, education, and celebration come together in a unique blend. And along the way, I met Eloisha, an extraordinary singer who wrote an afro hair anthem for children, a joyful chorus that turns self-love into song.

I discovered that in New York, the Natural Hairstyle & Braid Coalition (NHBC) is leading the charge to make sure natural hair care remains what it has always been—a safe, professional, and respected practice rooted in health, culture, and science. In 1993, New York made history as the first state in the US to establish a Natural Hair Care & Braiding License, setting a new national standard for recognizing natural hair care as both a skilled and legitimate profession.

Today, the NHBC, led by five visionary Black women in the natural hair industry, carries that legacy forward. They collaborate with legislators, educators, and local communities to uphold licensing standards that safeguard both stylists and clients.

The community that emerged from our work was unlike anything I had experienced before. It wasn't just about natural hair acceptance, though that was certainly part of it. It was about creating spaces where authenticity was celebrated, where our stories mattered, where our experiences were validated and valued.

In this community, when a woman shared that she had been told her locs were "unprofessional," she wasn't met with advice to conform or suggestions to "pick her battles." She was met with understanding, with anger on her behalf, and with practical support for fighting back. When someone posted pictures of their natural hair journey, they weren't asking permission to exist; they were claiming their right to be beautiful exactly as they were.

What does sisterhood and solidarity look like around natural hair? It appears that women are traveling across oceans to testify at legislative hearings on behalf of people they've never met. It appears to involve sharing research and resources across language barriers. It appears to be about celebrating each other's victories and supporting one another through defeats.

It looks like understanding that when one of us wins, we all win. When France passes legislation against hair discrimination, it sets a model for other countries. When the CROWN Act passed in American states, it provided advocates with legal language and strategies. When a woman in South Africa, Ghana, or anywhere else decides to challenge hair discrimination, she's building on the foundation that all of us have laid together.

The community also looks like honest conversations about the challenges we face within our own families and cultures. Because hair discrimination doesn't just come from white employers or European beauty standards—it also comes from within our own communities, from relatives who tell us to "do something with that hair" before job interviews, from peers who have internalized the same anti-Blackness that oppresses all of us.

Building this community has changed my relationship with myself in ways I couldn't have anticipated. Before, I felt isolated and uncertain. I questioned my own perceptions, wondered if I was being overly sensitive, and doubted whether my experiences were valid enough to warrant serious consideration.

However, being surrounded by women with similar stories, struggles, and strengths has given me unshakeable confidence in my truth. I know now that my experiences weren't isolated incidents or personal failings. They were part of a systematic pattern of discrimination that affects millions of people worldwide.

This community has also taught me that advocacy work is sustainable only when it's supported by collective action. I couldn't have pushed for legislative change on my own, no matter how passionate I was about it. I needed Lovely's inside knowledge of the political process. I needed Professor Greene's legal expertise, and I needed Mr. Serva to recognize its importance. I needed every woman who shared her story, every person who attended our hearings, and every voice that contributed to our chorus.

The work continues to grow. I've been invited to speak in Senegal next year, where I'll connect with artists and visit schools to discuss hair acceptance and self-love with young people. Communities are forming in countries I've never visited, advocates taking up this work in languages I don't speak, and young people growing up with more confidence and self-acceptance than my generation ever had.

Sometimes I think about that first moment when I read about Mr. Traoré in that French magazine, sitting in my apartment in Florida, feeling so alone and angry. I could never have imagined that individual moments of recognition would lead to this—an international community of advocates, a network of support that spans continents, and a movement that's still growing and evolving.

That's the power of community, finding your people, and discovering that your personal struggle connects to something much larger than yourself. You don't have to carry the weight of change alone. You don't have to fight these battles in isolation. Somewhere out there are people who understand your experience, who share your vision, who are willing to work alongside you to create the world you all deserve to live in.

The community of empowerment isn't just about natural hair, though that's where many of us started. It's about creating spaces where authenticity is valued over conformity, diversity is celebrated rather than merely tolerated, and every person can show up as their full self without apology or compromise.

And once you've experienced that kind of community, once you've felt that level of support and understanding, you can never go back to fighting alone. You become part of something bigger, something stronger, something that will continue long after any individual victory or defeat.

That's what real empowerment looks like, not just individual self-acceptance, but collective action that creates lasting change for everyone who comes after us.

Reflection Questions

1. **Discovering Your Tribe**: Change often starts with something personal. What experiences or passions in your life could help you connect with others who understand your journey? Where might you find those people—online, in your community, or through shared interests?
2. **Beyond Personal Boundaries**: Hair discrimination isn't limited to one group—it can affect anyone whose appearance doesn't fit narrow societal expectations. Think about challenges you've faced in your own life. How might they connect to larger social issues or shared experiences in your community?

Chapter 10: Becoming Whole Again

There is no final destination in this journey, only daily acts of self-love and resistance. If you've been waiting for me to tell you that one day you wake up completely healed, confident, or unbothered by the world's opinions about your hair, I'm going to disappoint you. That's not how this works. That's not how any of this works.

What I've learned through decades of struggle, years of advocacy, and countless moments of both triumph and doubt is this: becoming whole again isn't about reaching a place where you never question yourself. It's about building the strength to question everything else.

When I was that little girl in Guadeloupe, watching the women around me struggle with their own hair, I absorbed the message that something about us was fundamentally wrong. Not different, but wrong and deficient. Not beautiful in our own way, but ugly by the only standards that seemed to matter.

When I became that young woman sitting in salon chairs enduring chemical burns and hours of heat damage, I thought I was choosing beauty. I thought I was choosing acceptance. I thought I was choosing an easier path through a world that had already decided what professional, attractive, and worthy looked like.

When I became that professional woman hiding behind wigs and extensions, building a successful career while quietly erasing parts of myself, I told myself I was being practical. I told myself I was picking my battles. I told myself I was doing what I had to do to survive, to thrive, in spaces that weren't made for people like me.

But the truth I've learned, the truth I want to shout from every platform I'm given, is that all of those moments were part of a larger violence. Not physical violence, though the chemicals and heat damage certainly harmed our bodies. But psychological violence. Spiritual violence. The kind of systematic assault on your sense of self that happens so gradually, so consistently, so pervasively that you mistake it for normal.

The natural hair journey is not just aesthetic; it's also a personal and transformative experience. It's political because in a world where European features are centered as the standard of beauty and professionalism, choosing to wear your hair as it grows from your head is an act of rebellion. It's a refusal to participate in your own erasure. It's a declaration that you deserve to take up space exactly as you are.

It's spiritual because it forces you to confront generations of inherited trauma, to heal wounds you didn't create but that live in your body nonetheless. When you stop chemically processing your hair, cut away the damaged parts, and learn to care for your natural texture, you're not just changing your appearance; you're also embracing your true self. You're breaking cycles. You're reclaiming something that was taken from your ancestors and denied to your descendants.

And it's deeply, profoundly human because it asks the question that sits at the heart of every liberation movement: Who gets to define what is beautiful, valuable, worthy of love and respect? Who gets to decide what is professional, appropriate, and acceptable in the spaces where we work and learn, and live? And who suffers when we let them maintain that power?

I think about the little girl I was, and I want to travel back in time to tell her: You are not the problem. Your hair is not the problem. The problem is a world that has convinced you that your natural state needs to be fixed, managed, hidden, or changed. The problem is systems that profit from your insecurity, that benefit from your belief that you're not enough as you are.

I think about the young woman I became, and I want to shake her gently and say: Stop trying to make yourself smaller. Stop trying to make yourself more palatable. Stop trying to earn acceptance from people who have decided that people who look like you don't belong. Your energy is precious. Your creativity is valuable. Your voice is needed. Please don't waste any of it trying to become someone else's version of acceptable.

I think about the professional woman I was for so many years, and I want to remind her: Your success that was built on a foundation of self- denial was not true success. It was survival. And while survival is sometimes necessary, it should never be confused with thriving. You deserve to thrive. You deserve to succeed while being authentically, unapologetically yourself.

The journey from self-hatred to self-love, from conformity to authenticity, from isolation to community, is not linear. It's not simple. There are setbacks and breakthroughs, moments of clarity and periods of confusion, victories that feel too small and challenges that feel overwhelming.

Some days, even now, I look in the mirror and have to choose actively to see beauty instead of deficiency. Some days, the little girl who learned that her hair was wrong tries to whisper those lies back to me. Some days, the professional woman who survived by conforming tries to convince me that authentic self-expression is too risky, too radical, too much.

But here's what I know now that I didn't know then: those voices aren't mine. They never were. They're the voices of a world that needs me to stay small, stay quiet, stay compliant. They're the voices of systems that profit from my insecurity and benefit from my silence.

My voice, the real one, the true one, is the voice that said "no more" when I saw Mr. Traoré's story. The voice that demanded legislative action when I discovered the scope of hair discrimination. The voice that would not be silenced or overshadowed by people seeking credit for my work. The voice that continues to speak even when it shakes, even when it's challenged, even when it would be easier to stay quiet.

This voice doesn't just belong to me. It belongs to every woman who has ever been told her natural hair was unprofessional. It belongs to every child who has learned to hate what grows from their head. It belongs to every person who has been made to feel that their authentic self isn't acceptable in the spaces where they need to exist.

When I speak now, at conferences, in interviews, on stages around the world—I'm not just sharing my story. I'm sharing our story. The collective narrative of people who have been told we don't fit, who have been pressured to change ourselves rather than challenge the systems that exclude us.

The work I do as an advocate isn't separate from the work I do as an artist. Both are acts of creation, acts of imagination, acts of envisioning and building worlds that do not yet exist. When I create art that centers Black beauty and tell stories that challenge dominant narratives, I'm engaging in advocacy work. When I research discrimination, when I build coalitions, when I push for legislative change, I'm doing creative work.

Because at the end of the day, all of this is about imagination. It's about imagining a world where children grow up loving every part of themselves. It's about imagining workplaces where authenticity is valued over conformity. It's about imagining beauty standards that celebrate diversity rather than demanding uniformity.

The legislation we passed in French Congress is just the beginning. Not just because it still needs Senate approval, not just because similar laws need to be passed in other countries, but because changing laws is only the first step in changing culture. Laws can prohibit discrimination, but they can't mandate love. They can create consequences for bias, but they can't create appreciation for diversity. That deeper work, the work of transformation, happens in individuals, communities, families, schools, and workplaces, one conversation at a time, one person at a time, one choice at a time.

This is why the personal is political, why individual healing contributes to collective liberation, and why your decision to love yourself as you are is, in fact, an act of resistance. When you choose authenticity over acceptance, when you choose self-love over conformity, when you choose to challenge beauty standards rather than conform to them, you're not just changing your own life. You're changing the world for everyone who comes after you.

I want you to understand something: you don't need to become an advocate, an artist, or a public speaker to be part of this revolution. You don't need to start organizations, push legislation, or give interviews. You need to live authentically. You need to question the messages you've internalized about your own worth. You need to challenge systems that demand your compliance. You need to love yourself and encourage others to love themselves, exactly as you are.

Every time you wear your natural hair to a job interview, you're making space for the next person to do the same. Every time you refuse to accept discrimination as normal, you're creating possibilities for change. Every time you choose self-love over self-denial, you're modeling a different way of being for everyone watching.

The revolution happens in the mirror when you look at yourself and choose to see beauty instead of flaws. It happens in the workplace when you show up authentically and refuse to shrink. It happens in your family when you teach children to love themselves before the world teaches them not to. It happens in your community when you support others in their journeys toward self-acceptance.

Becoming whole again doesn't mean you were ever actually broken; it simply means you've found a way to heal. It means recognizing that you were taught to see yourself as broken, and choosing to unlearn those lessons. It means understanding that the problem was never you—it was a world that couldn't handle your full, authentic, beautiful self.

I am still becoming, learning, and growing. I continue to challenge myself to love more deeply, speak truthfully, and act courageously. The woman writing these words is not the same woman who started this journey, and she's not the final version either. That's the beauty of this work, it's never finished because we're never finished growing, learning, evolving.

But I know this: I will never again hide who I am to make others comfortable. I will never again accept discrimination as the price of participation. I will never again let anyone, including myself, convince me that my natural state needs to be fixed.

And I hope, no, I believe, that somewhere, someone reading this will make the same commitment. Someone will look in the mirror tomorrow and choose love over criticism. Someone will walk into a workplace and decide they deserve to belong exactly as they are. Someone will teach their children, students, or community that beauty comes in infinite forms, that professionalism has nothing to do with hair texture, that worthiness is not conditional on conformity.

The natural hair journey forces us all to question fundamental assumptions about beauty, about acceptance, about who gets to define worth in our society. Those questions don't have easy answers, but they're the right questions to ask. They're the questions that lead to liberation.

Who gets to define beauty? We do. All of us. Together. Who gets to decide what's professional? We do. By showing up authentically and demanding respect. Who suffers when we let others control these definitions? Everyone. Because when some people aren't free, none of us are truly free.

The revolution is not coming. It's here. It's happening every time someone chooses authenticity over acceptance, every time someone loves themselves before waiting for permission, every time someone refuses to participate in their own oppression.

You are part of this revolution whether you know it or not. Your choices matter. Your voice matters. Your authentic self matters.

The question is not whether you're worthy of love and acceptance as you are—you absolutely are. The question is whether you're ready to act like you believe it.

The world is waiting for your answer. And more importantly, you're waiting for your answer.

What will it be?

Final Reflection: Your Journey Forward

As you close this book and continue your own journey, carry these questions with you:

1. **What messages about yourself are you ready to unlearn?** What stories about your worth, your beauty, your acceptability have you been carrying that no longer serve you?

2. **Where in your life are you still seeking permission to be authentic?** What spaces, relationships, or situations still feel unsafe for your full self-expression?
3. **How will you contribute to creating the world you want to live in?** What small acts of resistance and self-love can you commit to practicing daily?

The revolution continues with you. In your choices. In your courage. In your commitment to loving yourself and others exactly as you are.

Welcome to becoming whole again. Welcome to coming home to yourself. Welcome to the revolution.

The Cover

The cover features a portrait of me at age six, with short hair and furrowed brows, an image from my childhood that poses the book's central question: Who defines our beauty? The haircut, imposed in the name of discipline rather than chosen, becomes a discreet emblem of control. My frown expresses silent resistance: A calm but firm "no" that refuses to be silenced. Combined with the text, the image invites us to embark on a journey: From imposed norms to chosen pride.

The orange and brown palette conveys the emotional charge. Orange is the pulse, the warmth, the boldness, the energy of metamorphosis. Brown is the ground, the earth, the skin, the anchor. Together, orange elevates and brown roots; one opens up the field of possibilities, the other remembers the origin. The palette expresses what the child could not yet articulate: Even when cut short, identity does not diminish, it germinates.

This portrait is not nostalgic. It is proof. The little girl with her hair cut short, her eyebrows furrowed in silent resistance, becomes the witness to the book's thesis and prepares the reader to enter this story with tenderness and courage.

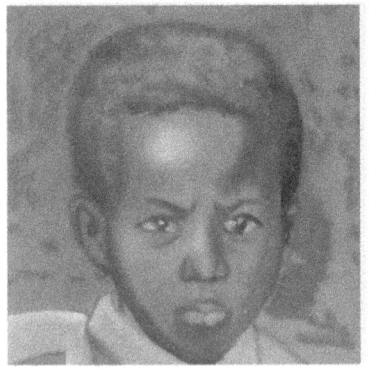 

About Guylaine Conquet

As a French figurative artist originally from Guadeloupe and now based in Atlanta, Georgia, Guylaine Conquet uses her art as a powerful vehicle for raising awareness about hair identity and self-acceptance. Her work is deeply inspired by her personal journey with natural hair—a transformation from feelings of shame and conformity to a celebration of beauty, resilience, and pride. Since 2019, she has been dedicated to exploring the history and cultural significance of Black hair, and challenging long-standing societal norms that have marginalized and stigmatized it.

Through vibrant colors, expressive textures, and bold symbolism, Conquet's paintings tell the stories of Black identity, heritage, and empowerment. Her art serves as a visual dialogue that encourages introspection and challenges Eurocentric beauty standards, highlighting the significance of hair as a marker of cultural pride and personal freedom.

Beyond her artistic practice, Conquet is a committed activist. She spearheaded the initiative that led to France's historic law against hair discrimination. Collaborating with MP Olivier Serva, she mobilized political leaders, community advocates, and the public to support legislative action, resulting in the landmark bill passed by French Parliament on March 28, 2024. This made France the first country in the world to implement a national law prohibiting discrimination based on hair.

Her influence extends beyond galleries and political spheres—she is a sought-after speaker at conferences, high schools, and universities, where she shares her insights on art, identity, and activism. Through both her words and her brushstrokes, she empowers others to embrace their heritage and reject discriminatory standards.